The Lord's Prayer

A Way of Life

DONALD W. SHRIVER, JR.

John Knox Press
ATLANTA

Library of Congress Cataloging in Publication Data

Shriver, Donald W., 1927-
  The Lord's prayer.

  Rev. ed. of: The social ethics of the Lord's prayer. 1980.
  Includes bibliograpical references and index.
  1. Lord's prayer—Addresses, essays, lectures.
I. Title.
BV230.S425   1983   226'.9606   83-9843
ISBN 0-8042-2409-9

Contents

Introduction   1

CHAPTER 1:
The Bond of Tender Supremacy   5

CHAPTER 2:
Food, Freedom, and Human Destiny   35

CHAPTER 3:
Our Hope for Community   71

CHAPTER 4:
On the Way to the Coming Kingdom   89

Notes   109

Index of Persons and Subjects   121

Index of Scripture References   125

To
MY MOTHER AND MY FATHER

Gladys Roberts Shriver
and
Donald Woods Shriver

who taught me the humanity of the Bible in their own

Introduction

The modern world likes to separate and distinguish. It is less skillful in relating things.

If we tag a person an "intellectual," for example, we think that he or she must not be very active or practical. Both "thinking" and "acting" we little associate with *prayer*, which for us is something "spiritual." People who write our movies, television programs, and newspapers have difficulty fitting prayer into their dramas, comedies, news stories. For many, prayer, if anything, is the subjective preoccupation of individuals. Observed from afar, prayer has little to do with thought, action, or society.

The viewpoint of this little book cuts across every one of these popular contemporary assumptions. It has to crosscut them; for it concerns the prayer taught to his disciples by a man whose life, as recorded in the New Testament, could never be summarized as devoted merely to personal piety, or to academic thought, or to action in society. Jesus of Nazareth does not fit ancient or modern stereotypes of the saint, intellectual, and politician. In his life, the records testify, thought, public activity, and prayer composed an exquisite whole. The role models of his and our own age did not fit him. From the standpoint of the Christian faith that has arisen in relation to him, he himself is the model for the remodeling of our humanity. In him God's intentions for humanity "became flesh and dwelt among us, full of grace and truth" (John 1:14).

As his earliest disciples were beginning to glimpse in him just such a fulfillment of their own humanity, they saw him at prayer one day, and one of them advanced a simple, urgent

request on behalf of all twelve of them: "Lord, teach us to pray
. . ." (Luke 11:1). His answer is the basis of this book, hundreds
of other books that have been written, hundreds yet to be written, and literally billions of prayers offered by Christians over
two thousand years of history.

Why another book on the Lord's Prayer? I have two reasons,
one general and the other quite specific. Anyone writing on any
subject as a Christian already has reason to pay careful attention
to the Lord's Prayer. This prayer, in Helmut Thielicke's phrase,
"spans the world."[1] It embraces the whole context of human life
from "heaven" to earth, from the creation of the universe to the
end of it, from today's gnawing hunger pangs to the great final
feast of history's end-time, from the wrongs that we daily visit
upon our human neighbors to the great onslaughts of evil that
await us in the future. "It would be possible to draw up an
account of all the Gospel teachings under the various heads of
the Lord's Prayer," said E.F. Scott.[2] Through the history of the
church it has been so used for introducing new Christians to
their gospel heritage. The "systematic theology" of the early
church was embodied chiefly, for the ordinary church member,
in three short statements—the Apostles' or Nicene Creed, the
Ten Commandments, and the Lord's Prayer. Since that early
time, theologians have routinely used one of the creeds as out-
line for their books. Ethicists have similarly used the Ten Commandments. Occasionally (as in Augustine's *Confessions*)
theologians have written about God in the form of prayerful
second-person address to God, but this has been a historical
exception. The idea of theology as a thoughtful working-out of
the meaning of prayer, in fact, has been rare.

Even rarer has been the idea that Christian ethics may be a
reflection on human social activity required by prayer. Yet this
idea is utterly consistent with everything Jesus taught. On the
whole we who try to be ethical teachers of the church have
neglected this principle, and that is my second, concrete reason
for this book. In my academic field of Christian Social Ethics we
have a reputation for being either very intellectual or very
activist, but seldom does anyone accuse us of being very prayer-

ful. Is it not high time to work on the connection between Christians-at-prayer and Christian behavior in the world? Should not that connection be made often in every era of the church? The aim of these pages is to encourage readers to pray this prayer of Jesus consciously in the context of the whole human world in which we now live. So to pray it requires much intellectual work in conjunction with much social-historical wisdom. So to pray it implies strong intention to "do the truth" of the prayer (John 3:21). Praying, thinking, and acting belong together: Christians must find ways to recover this comprehensive style of life from the message, ministry, and grace of our Lord Jesus, for whom prayer was "at once word, thought, and life."[3]

A further introductory note: this is the second version of this book to appear in print. The first was published in 1980 under the title, *The Social Ethics of the Lord's Prayer*, by the Christian Literature Society of Madras, India.[4] The four chapters here began as four lectures delivered to the annual Clergy Conference of the Mar Thoma Syrian Church of South India. This revision and expansion of those lectures, recast with American readers in mind, still bears the mark of that beginning. Nothing could be more appropriate to the subject matter. The community of Christians, the church, now spans the world, too. No concrete act unites us so routinely as our saying of "the prayer that Jesus taught us." The saying of this prayer is probably the most pervasive, ecumenical act of Christians down through the centuries. In almost every ecumenical gathering of church people which I have attended in my lifetime, the one thing that our clashing liturgical orthodoxies permitted was congregational utterance of this prayer. In multi-linguistic meetings the great ecumenical custom has been for each participant to pray it in his or her own language, producing a glorious hubbub spiritually akin to that recorded in Acts 2.

As a source of social ethics for American Christians, therefore, the Lord's Prayer comes to us ecumenically affiliated. These pages come so affiliated, and I am pleased to acknowledge my debt to those Christian friends of the Mar Thoma church who listened patiently, and, who with equal patience offered correction and encouragement to me when this exploration was first undertaken with them.

Fundamentally, one has to remember, this prayer belongs to Jesus, who meant for it to belong to the whole church. In no distinctive sense does it belong to the American section of that church—which is to forecast one of the ethical pressures to be experienced by anyone who dares to do the truth of this prayer.

When the substance of these pages was first shared with that gathering of clergy from South India, a number of them said to me that they had been praying the Lord's Prayer all their lives but that now the prayer had become harder for them to pray. It was harder for me, too, I confessed. When one consciously builds a bridge from prayer to reflection on the whole life of one's self, church, and society, routineness is indeed shattered. This can be a disturbing experience. But it can also introduce us anew to the central theme of the Gospel: the grace of the Lord Jesus Christ, the love of God and the community of the Holy Spirit, which alone permit and enable us to "pray like this" (Matt. 6:9). May the benediction rather than the burden of the Lord's Prayer come to rest upon readers of these pages.

CHAPTER 1

The Bond of
Tender Supremacy

In current American life, prayer is a public fact. Our customs call for prayer at football games, the opening of Congress, the inauguration of presidents, civic club lunches, and—many religious citizens insist—in public school classrooms. If the Apostle Paul came to modern-day America, he might well begin a speech as he began one to the ancient Athenians: "I perceive that in every way you are very religious" (Acts 17:22).

What is more truly a token of religion than prayer? What distinguishes practical from theoretical religion so surely as the practice of prayer? A higher power is only a theory if one never prays to him, her, or it. Indeed, the practice of prayer seems so ingrained in human experience that many avid secularists have difficulty, as they move from cradle to grave, avoiding something like prayer. Our English manners preserve for us the remnant of a prayer when we say, "Good-by" (God be with ye). Less mannerly and often more fervently, some of us employ the pseudo-prayer of profanity to express strong feeling, to call upon a deity to destroy this or that human project. More serious and closer to subjectively real prayer is the involuntary cry that rises from our lips under the first blow of catastrophic suffering: "O God!" And not long ago the head of the most powerful Marxist country in the world commented publicly that "God will not forgive us" if we—the Americans and the Soviets—fail to prevent nuclear war. Before he pressed the button to engage in such a war, might even Yuri Andropov utter a prayer of desperation to that higher power in which he is not supposed to believe?[1]

In view of this continued frequency of prayer among contemporary human beings, it is easy for us to understand why

Jesus spent little time telling his disciples that they should pray. Prayer was more or less everywhere in the culture of Jews and Gentiles of the day. The disciples themselves never seemed to have raised the question, "Why pray?" To them and to Jesus, the question-with-many-answers was, "*How* pray?" If we go to the two places in the New Testament where Jesus gives a direct answer to the question (Matt. 6:9–13 and Luke 11:1–4) we find, in the text and context, two striking preliminary answers.

Neither Long nor Lonely

In its ordinary form among humans, prayer consists of words. In New Testament teaching words can either be "empty" or "full of grace and truth."[2] Beware the customs of religion around you, Jesus said to the disciples in the collection of his teachings we call the Sermon on the Mount. Beware especially of the human attempt to persuade God to do something. At best, this is magic, at worst profanity, the product of an erroneous understanding of God:

> "In praying do not heap up empty phrases as the Gentiles do; for they think that they will be heard for their many words. Do not be like them, for your Father knows what you need before you ask him. Pray then like this. . . ." (Matthew 6:7–9a)

Prayer, Jesus demonstrates in the words following, begins and ends in adoration. Petitionary prayer, prompted in deep human need, should rise from our lips, like flowers under the sun, in grateful acknowledgment of an energy, a power already present and already making our existence and our prayer possible. As the Calvinists like to say, the chief purpose of being human is "to glorify God and to enjoy God forever." As Jesus goes on to say later in Matthew 6, *pagan* prayer can be distinguished from *faithful* prayer in the solidity of the latter's confidence in the power and the kindness of God the Creator. Persons who entertain a gnawing doubt about either the power or the kindness have reason to pray at great length, wordily. Perhaps, they think, the right words will add to God's disposition and ability to be kind!

Cut short any such theology of prayer in your minds, says Jesus. Be boldly brief and forthright in ascribing power and kindness to the One to whom you are about to pray. Do this in the first word by which you address that One.

We shall have much to consider in our reflections on this first word in the pages to follow. But another preliminary reflection about the second word in Matthew's Greek version of the Lord's Prayer: "our." We know from Luke's version[3] that the disciples, at some point, asked Jesus to "teach us to pray," and in both versions Jesus answers the request literally in regard to the "us." Repeatedly (nine times in Matthew and seven in Luke) some form of the word "we" is used, so that we can be sure that the Lord's Prayer was first and always meant to be the prayer of a community.[4]

At this point we American Christians have some recovery of our biblical heritage to attempt. That the Lord's Prayer should ever be uttered at a football game or in a public school classroom would have perplexed and astonished the people who first prayed "like this." They were a people who, in the first century A.D., invented a new word for their community, "church," the people of the Lord.[5] This was the Lord's Prayer, to be prayed by the the Lord's people, together. It is neither a public nor an individual prayer. It is a prayer of the church. As the lifelong example of Jesus suggests, there is a place for individual prayer among his disciples; but the model, the routine norm of prayer for us is *social*. Our ability to pray personally derives from our participation in the prayer of a community—a thought that individualistic American Protestants, with their suspicion of "organized worship" and "set prayers" are bound to find uncomfortable. Authentic prayer must be socially learned.

Our very ability to "pray like this" presupposes as much. Our knowledge of this prayer comes to us through the historical church and its labor of preservation of the Bible. Our ability to interpret the original meaning of the prayer and its meaning to us will always hinge on an understanding of its meaning to those early church people who first prayed it. In this book we shall often move back and forth between the One to whom this prayer is directed and the ones who pray this way. The two dimensions of the prayer belong together, each interprets the other. We shall not have drifted away from the first Greek word of the prayer ("Father"), then, if we turn for a moment to inquire about the historic human reality in the second—"our."

Who Were They Who First Prayed This Way?

A modern sociologist might describe the early Christians, as one group of humans among others, as "urban lower class." We know from the book of Acts and the letters of Paul some obvious reasons for such a designation. Paul was simply describing the social facts of the young church in Corinth, for example, when he said to its members:

> Consider your call, brethren; not many of you were wise according to worldly standards, not many were powerful, not many were of noble birth. (1 Corinthians 1:26)

Much the same could have been said of the earliest disciples of Jesus and of Jesus himself. As son of a carpenter, Jesus apparently was a skilled laborer. He knew how to read, and almost certainly the twelve disciples knew how to read, too. But in the years just ahead, the new Christian congregations of the Roman Empire were to fill up with more folk from the "low" side of the sociological-prestige scale than the high side. Low in that day, of course, had its firm measure in the status of the largest single class of people in the empire: slaves, who must have constituted a sizable proportion of the Christian community in cities like Corinth. The church there was surely not a province of highly civilized society, as Paul's correspondence makes clear. From the standpoint of what contemporary Greek and Roman culture considered civilization, in fact, the early Christian churches were hardly worth noticing. That is why one finds so little reference to their existence in the Greek and Roman historians of the time.

The impact of the gospel of Jesus Christ upon the world of Greece and Rome is complicated and uncertain. But scholars like C. N. Cochrane, Ernst Troeltsch, and Erich Auerbach have demonstrated that the impact involved, at the very least, a new philosophy about what was worth recording in human history books. In the civilized view of the time, common people were not the makers of history. "The powerful and the noble-born" were its makers. No foot soldier, house slave, street sweeper, fisher, or carpenter deserves a place in the collective memory of the human race. Such people are not capable of playing heroic parts on the stages of history. If they come on stage momentarily, they do so for purposes of comedy. One cannot take them as fully serious human beings. As Auerbach says, commenting on the New Testament story of Simon Peter:

> It takes place entirely among everyday men and women of the common people; anything of the sort could be thought of in antique terms only as farce or comedy. Yet why is it neither of these? Why does it arouse in us the most serious and most significant sympathy? Because it portrays something which neither the poets nor the historians of antiquity ever set out to portray: the birth of a spiritual movement in the depths of the common people, from within the everyday occurrences of contemporary life, which thus assumes an importance it could never have assumed in antique literature. What we witness is the awakening of a "new heart and a new spirit." All this applies not only to Peter's denial but also to every other occurrence which is related in the New Testament. Every one of them is concerned with the same question, the same conflict with which every human being is basically confronted and which therefore remains infinite and eternally pending. . . . What we see here is a world which on the one hand is entirely real, average, identifiable as to place, time, and circumstances, but which on the other hand is shaken in its very foundations, is transforming and renewing itself before our eyes.[6]

In short, the good news that came to human beings in Jesus implied a revolution in our assessment of each other's worth. In this gospel lay planted the seeds of dispute with any social ideology that divided humans between "upper" and "lower." Now that "the light which enlightens every man" (and woman and slave! John 1:9) had come into the world in Jesus of Nazareth, risen from the dead, no human person was unimportant or unrelated to the great kingdom of God, the Creator and Savior of the world. No matter how limited, selective, and partial a human history book would always be, there is a history of which God is author and finisher, and to this history every human can belong. Every human person: identified and marked out for the love of One who made the universe! In this new understanding of human existence, Paul was not exaggerating when he said to the Corinthian Christians:

> God has chosen things low and contemptible, mere nothings, to overthrow the existing order. And so there is no place for human pride in the presence of God. You are in Christ Jesus by God's act, for God has made him our wisdom; he is our righteousness; in him we are consecrated and set free. (1 Corinthians 1:28–30, NEB)

When we think about the people who first prayed their Lord's Prayer, we should remember particular persons named in the New Testament—Peter, John, Andrew, Mary, Martha, Lydia, Priscilla, Aquila, Onesimus, Philemon, Rufus, Junias, Timothy, Fortunatus, Tychicus, Epaphroditus—and dozens of other *nobodies* in the history of earth who became *somebodies* by the grace of God in Jesus Christ.

Such somebodies were the first to pray the Lord's Prayer. Joy and gratitude over their new status, as objects of the love that had confronted them in Jesus, well up in them as they pray. They are a people of *this* One to whom Jesus prayed, in whom he trusted even to death, by whom he was raised from the dead, and into whose kingdom he welcomed the "least" and the "greatest" of them, so abolishing that prideful distinction.

The glory of that gospel shone in a word that Jesus chose to designate that One who has established forever the value of human beings. It is the word, "Father."

To Whom Did They Pray?

Finding the right name for something greatly concerned the ancient Hebrew. Early creation stories in Genesis portray the naming of all created things as a distinctive task of humans. But nowhere does the Hebrew Bible suggest that humans have the freedom to name their Creator, who is a self-namer. To "know the name of God" is to have been favored with God's own self-introduction, not as a fact to be observed in nature but in an encounter initiated by another, as when someone calls at your door. The Hebrew carried this sense of self-revelation over into an understanding of encounters of humans in society. Ignorance of each other's names keeps two or more people distant from each other. Once we know another's name, we have a relation of some intimacy. We can never be quite the same again; for, in possessing the name of another, we possess something of the core of his or her personhood. Names are serious matters. Unlike a removable tag or title, they are part of the reality they signify. Not just veneer, they are part of the solid wood.

The freedom to call God by just any name, therefore, no pious Hebrew could claim. More than one name for God abounded in the tradition, and one of the names (represented by the four Hebrew letters יהוה) was so sacred, so associated with divine self-revelation, that only the High Priest, once a year, was permitted to say it out loud. Thus removed from utterance by the lips of ordinary people, the name of God could be protected—but at the price of threatening the belief among those ordinary people that they were personally and directly related to their Creator. Without a name, God remains a stranger. With a name God is addressable.

Among the various steady impressions which Jesus left upon his followers, none was steadier than his naming of the world's Creator: *Father*. It was not the first time in the history of the Hebrew people that this word had been used to designate God. Nor was it the first time that analogies to human parenthood had been used to describe the power and kindness of the Lord of Israel's history:

> When Israel was a child, I loved him,
> and out of Egypt I called my son. . . .
> it was I who taught Ephraim to walk,
> I took them up in my arms. (Hosea 11:1,3)

Twice in the latter chapters of our book of Isaiah the prophet uses the term "Our Father" of the nation itself:

> Thou art our Father . . .
>   our Redeemer from of old is thy name." (Isaiah 63:16)

> O LORD, thou art our Father;
>   we are the clay, thou art our potter. (Isaiah 64:8)

But on the whole, the Old Testament rarely uses the word to designate God. Nowhere does it offer a precedent for an individual to call God by the term, "My Father"; nor does the phrase "Our Father" have a routine place in the public liturgy of the synagogue or temple during the time of Jesus.[7] It was quite otherwise in the new Christian church. "Father" was Jesus' most characteristic address to the world's Creator; and "Our Father" was *the* name by which the disciples came to participate in the same address. Indeed, twice in Paul's letters (Rom. 8:15 and Gal. 4:6) we see that the most primitive, basic prayer of Christians was the very Aramaic word with which Jesus himself must have begun the prayer taught the disciples: *abba*. Since most early Christians spoke Greek exclusively, this takeover of one Aramaic word into their spontaneous spiritual vocabulary is truly remarkable. We have every reason to believe that they borrowed the word directly from Jesus, by his express encouragement and example. Not only did they hear him use the phrase "my Father" in conversation and teaching about his relation to God, but they remembered most indelibly that in the moment of his own most agonizing prayer in Gethsemane, his address to God was simply, *abba* (Mark 14:36).[8]

While not a new name for God, therefore, *abba* on the lips of Jesus expressed a new combination of authority and intimacy, supremacy and closeness, awe and trust in the relation of humans to their Creator. This was the right name for the divine, the right word for the start of prayer. If they were to pray in the spirit and in the truth of Jesus' own prayers, his disciples had to accept his invitation to take the same name on their own lips. In many ways they were only too different from him; but in this one way at least, they were bold to be exactly like him: they addressed the great Creator of the universe, the Lord of Israel, as *abba*, the Father of the Lord Jesus.

To Whom Shall We Pray?

The word "Father" is now so routine in the interior life of the Christian churches of the world that we will need much study of this now ancient tradition—and fervent prayer!—if we are to appropriate the word with that ancient combination of respect and kinship between the human and the divine. For the early Christian, *abba* embodied a miracle: God is now with us in great power and compassion! This good news answers a central human anxiety which all religions, to some extent, seek to answer: in and behind the power we confront in the world around us, does that power, or its source, care for us? In the energies discovered by modern physics or the ravenous "black holes" evident now to astronomy, is there anything friendly to the likes of us mundane humans? The southern writer, James McBride Dabbs, said that in his childhood on a farm he often puzzled over the relationship between "the god of the fields" and the "god of hearth." The one was a power of awesome effect, for good and bad, on the lives of humans: sunshine and rain, drought and flood, new-sprouted cotton and boll weevil. The other seemed addressable under the family roof, intimate, warm, and at home with us. "The god of the fields was strong, but of not entirely proved goodness; the god of the fireside was good, but of doubtful strength and staying power."[9]

Making a connection between the two "gods" remains a classic focus of religion, and nothing in twentieth-century experience makes that focus out of date. Perhaps the twentieth century gives us larger reason than ever to ask the question of our significance in the world. Someone has said that few of us humans have the courage to stand outside under a starry sky and to shout our names to that sky. Modern astronomy, in particular, makes such a gesture seem ridiculous. So also does evolutionary thought with its uncovering of time spans in the millions and billions of years. Does the whole human species really amount to much in the whole scheme of things? The agnostic philosopher Max C. Otto spoke to this anxious question when he bravely proposed that "we acknowledge ourselves adrift in infinite space on our little earth, the sole custodians of our ideals."[10]

We must not overrate our distinctly modern vulnerability to such a belief. A large universe is not much lonelier than a large crowd of other humans who show no signs of caring for you. Different religions have their different ways of dealing with this endemic human concern, but almost all seek to proclaim that at least some of our "ideals" have a stronger "custodian" than ourselves. Wilbur Daniel Steele wrote a short story, "The Man Who Saw Through Heaven," on this very theme. In this story, an American man, innocent of any study of modern astronomy, goes to Africa as a Christian missionary. There he reads a book about the enormity of our multi-galactic universe, and his simple faith in "the god of the hearth" collapses. The little planet earth, he muses amid the ashes of his faith, is no more than a ring on the finger of a giant. How could the Creator of this monstrous universe pay any attention to so trivial a detail? After a long spiritual and physical pilgrimage, he stumbles his way back to an enlarged version of his faith; and he ends up carving an image of a giant humanlike figure bending over a ring on his finger. Before his death, African villagers for miles around have learned from him about "Our Father Witch." On his death bed, the missionary had learned to pray anew, "Our Father which art in heaven. . . ."[11]

On the relationship between the god of creative power and the god of infinite care, Jesus was an orthodox Hebrew theologian. Only a power great enough to preside over the fields and intimate enough to preside at the human hearth can be worshiped and trusted as God indeed. His assurances to his disciples here called their attention to the meaning of certain facts in the world of nature or in their memory of their own history. These early hearers of his teaching were poor people for the most part. They were little troubled by the stars but much troubled by starvation. Death stares poor people in the face every day of their lives; cold and hunger are their most convincing experience of a loveless universe. Take care, Jesus tells them according to Matthew 6:26–30, that you do not overestimate the theatening side of your experience. Today you woke up with the blood running warm in your veins.[12] You have some food in the pantry, some clothes on your backs; you survive, as the flowers and the birds survive for the moment. All this is the work of "your heavenly Father," Creator and sustainer of all that is. And you who know of the Creator's special care for an enslaved people in Egypt, do you not have "all the more" reason to believe in such a Creator?

If there was a new "argument" for the unity of the God of power and the God of loving kindness in Jesus, that argument was not in a verbal teaching but in the disciples' experience of the whole life, death, and resurrection in Jesus himself. It was one thing for him to teach the idea that the power who made the world can be trusted to sustain us in life and in death. It was another for the disciples to hear him commit himself to the Father in his own death-agony on the cross (Luke 23:46). H. Richard Niebuhr echoes the wonderment of this experience among disciples of all ages when he wrote that "the greatness and the strangeness of Jesus' love of God appear ... in his loyalty to the transcendent power that to all men of little faith seems anything but fatherlike."[13] The authority and authenticity of *abba*, as a name for God, for Christians early and late, roots in the confidence with which Jesus uttered it in his life, death, and resurrection-from-the-dead. The unity of divine power and love was revealed most notably in the ressurection. *This* was the great new fact celebrated in the New Testament. It was the heart of the good news: "This Jesus God raised up, and of that we all are witnesses!" (Acts 2:32).

This good news of the powerful, personal, caring presence of God in the world sounds with joy in the Lord's Prayer as repeated by the early Christians in their homes, church meetings, and celebrations of the Lord's Supper.[14] Now they could address the power behind the universe as "Father," not simply because of the ambiguous facts of the natural world; not only because once in Egypt that God showed astounding power and care towards a struggling slave people; but chiefly because Jesus, risen from the dead, was present with them in the Spirit. That Spirit put on their lips the word that he had taught them, enabling them too

> to cry "Abba! Father!" In that cry the spirit of God joins with our spirit in testifying that we are God's children. (Romans 8:16, NEB)

Human words are fragile containers for the treasure of God's presence in the world; but it is no exaggeration to say that the word *abba*, as used among the early Christians in prayer, embodied fully the good news that nothing "in all creation, will be able to separate us from the love of God in Christ Jesus our Lord" (Rom. 8:39). Here was a name by which God came as Self-introducer to every human door. Here, in a word, was the sign, seal, and first touch of God's presence to the human community. The ensuing, adoring petitions to follow, in the Lord's Prayer, reverberate with the immediacy, scope, and joy inherent in this gracious word:

> Let your great name, Father, be rightly uttered throughout the earth, and may we begin now to utter it in the power of our Lord Jesus!

> Let your rule come on earth in completion of what has already come to us in him and in your Spirit—in completion of your rule already begun in his life, death, and resurrection!

So to paraphrase the opening of the Lord's Prayer is to suggest that throughout the prayer echo meanings already implicit in *abba*. We stand already in the divine presence, if we so much as begin to pray like this. By accepting the privilege of uttering this name for our Creator and Sustainer, we step into family, the family of God, confessing that we are already God's beloved children.

His, Her? Father, Mother?

The miracle of the first word of the Lord's Prayer can be illuminated yet further if we conclude with a note on recent scholarly research on this word. Scholars are not in agreement on how the word was used during and soon after Jesus' time; but the most extensive combination of research and speculation about the word comes from Joachim Jeremias, who writes:

> The church fathers Chrysostom, Theodor of Mopsuestia, and Theodoret of Cyrrhus who originated from Antioch (where the populace spoke the West Syrian dialect of Aramaic) and who probably had Aramaic-speaking nurses, testify unanimously that *abba* was the address of the small child to his father. And the Talmud confirms this when it says: "When a child experiences the taste of wheat [i.e. when it is weaned], it learns to say *abba* and *imma* ["dear father" and "dear mother"]. *Abba* and *imma* are thus the first sounds which the child stammers. . . . *Abba* was an everyday word, a homely family word, a secular word, the tender . . . address [of the child] to its father: "Dear Father." . . . Jesus thus spoke with God as a [child speaks] with his father, simply, intimately, securely, [childlike] in manner. But his invocation of God as *abba* is not to be understood merely psychologically, as a step towards growing apprehension of God. Rather we learn from Matthew 11:27 that Jesus himself viewed this [childlike] form of address for God as the heart of that revelation which had been granted him by the Father. In this term *abba* the ultimate mystery of his mission and his authority is expressed. He, to whom the Father had granted full knowledge of God, had the messianic prerogative of addressing him with the familiar address of a [child].

Furthermore and more astonishing yet says Jeremias:

> In the Lord's Prayer Jesus authorizes his disciples to repeat the word *abba* after him. He gives them a share in his sonship and empowers them, as his disciples, to speak with their heavenly Father in just such a familiar, trusting way as a child would with his father. . . . Children can say '*abba*'! Only he who, through Jesus, lets himself be given the childlike trust which resides in the word *abba* finds his way into the kingdom of God.[15]

Scholarly caution about Jeremias' historical conclusions on this point is partly an echo of theological caution. Is there not a danger that the human who accepts the privilege of calling God by this intimate name will lose the awe and reverence of true prayer? The Roman Catholic Mass has long sought to preserve a note of awe and to guard against human presumption in its priestly introduction to the Lord's Prayer: "Taught by our Savior's command and formed by the word of God, we dare to say: 'Our Father. . . .' "

Between the infinite holiness and the infinite tenderness of "the Father," there seems to be an abiding tension. What is to prevent us from thinking that we have permission now to be chummy with the Maker and Sustainer of the universe? Here we modern Christians may need some help, not only from the Bible but from contemporary science. The mathematician J. B. S. Haldane once remarked that "the universe is not only queerer than we suppose, it is queerer than we *can* suppose."[16] So, all the more, the universe's Creator: unimaginably powerful, holy, and loving. There is a "critical rule" for our theology here: in defining the mystery of God, be careful that you neglect neither the awesome greatness nor the tender intimacy! Remember both the cross and the resurrection of Jesus! There love became powerful and power is loving, as nowhere else in the history of earth. This is what you are to remember when you "pray like this . . . ."

But there is another, similar caution that must be sounded in any late twentieth-century study of the Lord's Prayer. In recent years the caution has come especially from women in the church who ask the perfectly justified question: "Why 'Father' rather than 'Mother'?" This question, for its answer, will require more scholarship, theology, ethics, and liturgical experiment in the modern church than has yet been undertaken. But in this book on the social ethics of the Lord's Prayer, we confront a great question of human society in this same word that, according to Jesus, confronts us with the power and tender love of God. Did Jesus mean to tell us that God is more like a father than a mother? Are men and things masculine somehow closer to God and things divine than women and things feminine?

In order to wrestle with this question with theological integrity, modern Christians must take their due share of the task of theology itself: to relate what we accept as truth from the past to what we accept as truth in the present. These two are not always the same or easy to relate consistently. What follows is an attempt by this author, a man, to participate perhaps haltingly, in such a theological task.

Karl Barth raised a basic objection to much human thinking about God by protesting against our tendency, through human history, to elevate some portion of human experience—the rising sun, an ancient tree, dreams, or parenthood—to the status of a symbol of God. "God is like a father," we say casually—until we meet some young person from a broken home to whom the word means neglect, absence, abuse, or some other experience of love-lessness. Then theological reflection sets in, as we revise our first thought: "No, God is like a *good* human father." And then, some of us fair-to-middling fathers get uncomfortable with our only-too-plain fatherly faults. We are pushed by respect for both the goodness and the greatness of God to a more desperately faithful theological statement bordering on prayer: "May God be a father in far better ways than am I! And may my fatherhood repent and learn in the presence of his!" As Barth would put it, we are moving in this series of statements away from an "analogy of being" towards an "analogy of faith." The former **peers** at God through the lens of some bit of our experience. The latter peers at our experience through the lens of something dependable that God has already communicated to us in a self-revelation.

In recent years feminist theologians have raised important questions about this drift of Barthian interpretation of theological language. They grant that not everything associated with our experience of any human word should be associated with the One to whom Jesus prayed; but precisely in their human-ness, do any of our words ever lose some basic common-sense, historic meanings? As one Old Testament scholar, Phyllis Trible, puts the question: "Where in the theology of God the father is there room for the image of God, male *and female*?" And she goes on to comment:

> To say that God as God is neither male nor female is not to elim-inate sexuality from the symbols that we employ to talk of God. Further, to the extent that those symbols are predominantly male symbols, to that extent they evince a "sexist" bias, whether intentional or not.[17]

This modern discussion among Christian theologians, of course, is only possible because they agree on a basic rule for theological thinking in the Hebrew-Christian tradition: one must forever distinguish between God as revealed to us and the words which a tradition uses to express the revelation. The "treasure" of divine self-revelation comes to us in "earthen vessels" (2 Cor. 4:7) like the apostolic church and the Bible itself. John Robinson was speaking of the Bible when he told the Pilgrims departing from Plymouth in 1620 that "God has yet more light and truth to break forth from his holy word." Using that working-rule, many students of the Bible, especially the women among them, are asking the spiritual descendents of Robinson to look again at what may be implied in the very phrase "his" word. Those parts of the Christian movement like Calvinism, which have always stressed the importance of perpetual Bible study under the interpretive guidance of the Holy Spirit, should find this rule historically congenial. (It is sometimes forgotten among Calvinists that one of their great historical documents, the Westminster Confession, was the product of a group of theologians quite sure that they needed more "light" from the Spirit if they were to re-understand the Bible accurately and adequately for their own time, 1643–1645.)[18]

There are old questions about the meaning of the Bible that need to be asked again, and new questions which hardly any reader has asked prior to our time. As an example of the former type of question: why were the Old Testament writers so wary of suggesting that the God of Israel is either male or female in some unambiguous sense? The reason was the clarity of certain surrounding religions on the matter. Many understood their gods as having "fathered" or "given birth" to their respective tribal worshipers in a rather straightforward biological sense. The divine self-disclosure to Abraham and Moses called for quite a different description of Israel's beginnings. God was the one who "chose" Abraham, "called" Israel, and "elected" it to live in special covenant with its Redeemer-Creator, who acted in great power and love to deliver this people from their slavery in Egypt. The relation between God and

people here was effected through mutual choice, historical deci-
sion, and ongoing covenant with each other. Alongside Yahweh
the gods and goddesses of Cannaan were "other gods" indeed.
Where the Old Testament writers use their predominantly male
images of God, the distinction remains important to them, and
the recurring female images come out of the same covenantal
context of thinking. The female images are less frequent than
the male, but they are more common and more striking than
some of us have supposed, and feminist scholars have been
rightly calling all this to our attention.[19]

The teaching of Jesus depends deeply upon the whole Old
Testament tradition. It is not surprising that his language for
referring to God should be predominantly associated with maleness. But we need to remember the freedom with which he pictures God in all sorts of images and stories, especially in his
parables. Alongside the father of the Prodigal Son in Luke 15
hastens the woman in search of a lost coin. The response of the
first Christians to the teachings and ministry of Jesus was little
centered on this question, to be sure. At least we have no
records in the New Testament that women felt "put down" by
Jesus' use of the word *abba* rather than *imma* in his address to
God in prayer. (Our lack of records does not prove that they
did not have these feelings, however.) What does seem clear,
beginning in the churches described in Acts and the letters of
Paul, is that in this church, which early took the Lord's Prayer
into its worship, innumerable women did experience the liberation of the good news that "there is neither Jew nor Greek . . .
slave nor free . . . male nor female; for you are all one in Christ
Jesus" (Gal. 3:28). This summary declaration of Paul testifies to
this apostle's recognition that something radically new had happened in Jesus to challenge contemporary Jewish and Gentile
cultural standards for classifying human beings. Paul knew that
the Holy Spirit, who had called him to Macedonia, took him to
Lydia and other women who became the first Christians of Philippi. And he undertook various ministries in the young
churches where he was assisted not only by men like Aquila but
also by women like Priscilla (cf. Acts 16:13–15; 18:1–4, 18).

If we can believe that the Holy Spirit effected these "break-throughs" for the dignity of women in the New Testament church, how do we explain the many evidences of women's second-class status even in that church? After all, either Paul or a writer who came to be associated with him lays down the rule that women "should not speak in church" (1 Cor. 14:34; 1 Tim. 2:11–12). One explanation is old in church history: the church was slow to learn, slow to repent, slow to catch up with "all that Jesus began to do and teach" (Acts 1:1). Along the centuries of that history, it has done some catching up—as when the rule against women's speaking in church and the rule against their ordination as ministers were set aside as not truly compatible with the higher rule: "there is neither . . . male nor female . . . in Christ Jesus"!

A Roman Catholic feminist theologian, Catharina Halkes, points to this tension between the teachings of Jesus and the practices of the churches from the very earliest New Testament times. For example, she says,

> Jesus admonished his disciples not to call any man their father on earth, "for you have one Father, who is in heaven." (Matt. 23:9). This is a fundamental criticism of one man's domination of another, of men's domination of women in particular—in the churches as well. In this statement Jesus presents us with the paradigm of sisters and brothers in reciprocity. But as long as we accept Holy Fathers, Reverend Fathers, fathers confessor and conciliar fathers in our Church, we are ignoring the word of Scripture.[20]

The active ministry of Jesus in relation to women is the source of more powerful tension yet with the practices of the historic church. As many scholars point out, Jesus incurred the violent antagonism of powerful people in his society for a reason less related to theology than to the way in which that society rank-ordered its members: this man from Nazareth was stubbornly insisting on keeping company with the least prestigious people, "the least of these my brethren"—*and* sisters.

> Against all custom (and in violation of specific injunctions) he made women his friends, taught them Torah ([the Law], Luke

10:38–42), spent time with them in public and in private, and entrusted to them his single most important task, the witness to his Resurrection. The price he paid for this fearless love was his own life; and before that final reckoning he lost his family and his respectability (Mark 3:31–35). He was crucified because he contravened the religious law in the name of God who gave the law. His contraventions were all in favor of those whom the law oppressed—the "people of the land" who were ritually unclean in their daily work, the whores and tax officials who collaborated with the occupation forces, the women and children who were at the disposal of their men. The heart of his message, in word and deed, was that God is a father who frees us from oppression by including us in his family; that when God's will is done on earth all will be included and none excluded; that his fatherly care means equal dignity and worth for all. This message was a threat not only to the interests of a religion that used the law to establish an elite, but also to a society which used religion to oppress the weak. The impulse that went out from Jesus caused him to be crucified; it is not surprising that his followers tempered it to their times.[21]

Temper it they did. Temper it we do! Early and late in its history the Christian movement makes compromises between the will of its Lord and the standards of its surrounding cultures. Early, we have the establishment of all-male priesthoods and selective reading of the Bible to interpret human sexuality as somehow evil, especially in its female manifestastion. Late, we have Christian churches furnishing only trickles of support for granting votes to women, furnishing Victorians with theological reasons for "keeping women in the home," and looking askance on women who take leadership roles in the professions, government, and the church.

We need not respond to this sober history with despair and guilt at the perpetual falling-short of every generation of church people. What if the Spirit who raised Jesus were *not* forever agitating the historic church to perpetual reformation? Let us rejoice in the refusal of this Spirit to be domesticated and institutionalized in worship and church politics! One can even read the Old Testament, as Rosemary Ruether reads it, as the antagonism between "two religions"—the religion that fortifies

human custom and the religion that challenges it. Whether we
can dispense with both relations of religion to society, and
whether it is biblically accurate to speak of two (or only two)
religions in Hebrew and Christian history, remain open questions. But there is no doubt which of the two emphases the
prophets of Israel represented—they were challengers of culture, all of them. Jesus too was such a challenger. As Catharina
Halkes says, he challenged male-dominated cultural custom in
his very "association with women" and in this association there
was a new revelation that would remain unfulfilled, in its implications for society and the church, for centuries. "His followers
are entrusted with the task of making God's revelation more
explicit and of developing it at every period of history in a very
concrete form through the Spirit of Christ."[22]

So we come back anew to the question of Jesus' own word
for addressing God in prayer: does the "Spirit of Christ," so
restlessly at work "[setting] at liberty those who are oppressed"
(Luke 4:18) and so particularly present in the ministry of Jesus,
direct us now to reexamine our use of the word "father" for
God? Should we eliminate the word from our worship? Or is
there a way to continue using it while becoming free of the ever-
so-subtle suggestion that femaleness is not as "close" to God as
maleness? Not to *hear* this question, as it is posed by women in
the church today, may be not to be open to the moving of the
Spirit in our midst. It may also be not to pray, in spirit and in
truth, the very first petition of the Lord's Prayer: "Hallowed be
thy name." With ancient Hebrew prayer, Jesus bids us here to
pray in the passive voice. Who are we to believe that we can
rightly hallow the divine name in our use of any human word,
even one taught us by Jesus? In a world that tramples on the
divine, is always cheapening holy things, and always taking
God's names in vain, we have to acknowledge our dependence
upon God to achieve everything we pray for—beginning with a
right utterance of the divine name. As a human sound, the
word *abba* will not achieve it. Now and forever we must believe
that

the Spirit helps us in our weakness; for we do not know how to pray as we ought, but the Spirit himself intercedes for us with sighs too deep for words. (Romans 8:26)

We must rely on that Spirit for our understanding, in new ways, of Romans 8:26, too! The Spirit "himself"? In the original Greek, it turns out, the word "Spirit" is neuter, and one could translate, "the Spirit itself." Does that translation not obscure the personal reality of the Spirit? Might we not speak better of "the Spirit herself"? It would be a bit of justice to women in the church, perhaps, if—after a long tradition of blithe translation of the neuter for Spirit as "him"—we changed the tradition for the forseeable future to the female designation of the Spirit. And the step from here to the prayer, "Our Mother who art in heaven . . ." is not a long one. Should the contemporary church take that step?

This is not a comfortable suggestion for many in the church today, women as well as men. Not only does such a substitution seem to "challenge Jesus with Jesus," but it may inadvertently tempt us with a new level of idolatry of words. Prayer springs from the working of a Spirit too deep to be described by our words; it rises to the One who is "above all that we ask or think" (Eph. 3:20, KJV). Our words are important, but if we make them the *most* important issue in the church, we may be lured away from the very reverence that is the only true root of prayer. The caution here applies to every Christian who has thought about the question under discussion here: those who don't really want to discuss it, those who want very much to discuss it, those who stick firmly to "father" language for God, and those who are repelled by that language. One and all, we have to help protect each other from idolatry. As Christians we have that protection, we believe, in the Spirit moving in our midst, who moved Jesus and raised him from the dead. Idolatry means attributing holiness to some object apart from its relation to One who alone is holy. Divorced from its context of the teachings and ministry of Jesus, divorced from the gospel of the cross and resurrection, the very word *abba* can become an idol.

Divorced from that context, it can serve, as idols often do, to justify injustice. Set again and again in that context, all things human can take on new, more faithful forms.

One can sum up this discussion of a first, ethical issue at stake in a modern praying of the Lord's Prayer, as follows: human minds need comparisons—analogies—if they are to understand the scarcely understandable. God's stooping to the needs of our creaturely minds is part of the divine compassion at the heart of the whole idea of revelation. As vehicles for our encounter with that compassion, words with both female and male associations are much to be desired, and as many words as we can ever invent or discover for helping to bear so precious a treasure. Three feminist theologians put the central point here very well when they say:

> In Judaism and Christianity, God can never be fully known or named. At best, the "names" point to mystery and transcendence. Thus, since all language about God is inadequate, a variety of images, rather than a single kind, may witness more fully to the ineffable One and hence also reflect more authentically the experiences of all humankind.[23]

Shall we, then, continue to use the Lord's Prayer, and its opening address, "Our Father," in the contemporary church? To the surprise of some Christians in the pews on Sunday mornings, not all theologians, male and female, are ready to answer a clear "yes" or "no." Some have suggested that we change the phrase to "Our Parent," but the suggestion falls like a thud on the ears of many, for it seems to make God into an abstraction, damaging the intimacy side of the tenderness-and-supremacy which Jesus implied in the word. Who among us ever quite loses the echo of what it once meant to address our parents concretely—*abba*, *imma*, poppa, momma?

On the linguistic level alone, there would appear to be no clear answer to this contemporary question of liturgical practice. The solution really does belong to the realm of the Spirit, in the understanding and intentions that accompany any authentic prayer in the life of the community that prays. It *is* high time that men in church inquired into the spiritual dangers of exclusive preoccupations with male imagery for God. It *is* high time that all church people, women and men, reappropriated those aspects of Jesus' ministry that make abundantly clear his own break with many a male-supremancy assumption of his society. It is high time, in short, that we followed the leading of the Spirit away from all those elements in our religious forms that hinder women and men together from experiencing "the glorious liberty of the children of God" (Rom. 8:21). Where this Spirit is, there will be freedom (2 Cor. 3:17), including the freedom, in the church, to struggle toward new ways of affirming all its members as members indeed.

So, whether we are learning to say "Father" with a sense of the rightness of saying "Mother," too, or are learning to say "Mother" without denying that God can use analogies of fatherhood in spite of our misunderstanding of the same, we shall indeed have to be: *learners*, all of us; and all of us, *teachers* as well. Catharina Halkes is right to see, for every period of church history, a task for all its members: "making God's revelation more explicit and developing it . . . in a very concrete form through the Spirit of Christ." That Spirit is the final tester of all talk in the church, a principle that applies both to what we say and how we say it—to each other. We are called, says the New Testament, to "speak the truth in love" (Eph. 4:15). If we neglect the "how" of love, we may never arrive at the "what" of truth. The church exists as that body of folk who are convinced that nothing —not the inadequacy of human language nor the injustices of human society—shall "separate us from the love of God in Christ Jesus our Lord." The joy of that truth will always deserve the best words we can muster—and much loving struggle among us as to which words, in truth, are the best.

If We Begin to "Pray Like This"

The individual petitions of the Lord's Prayer seem constantly opening out to the prayer as a whole. In our struggle to understand the theological and ethical meanings of *abba*, we have already had to consider questions of the human inclusiveness of the prayer; and in petitions to come we shall be in the midst of language that obviously concerns the human side of the divine-human encounter—bread, sin, and temptation. From the first word of the prayer, with its pronoun—"Father of us"— we are learning to pray in a neighborhood of equal human persons. Before we advance to the other petitions (via consideration of what it means to pray "Thy kingdom come"), let us summarize here some history. Ethically and socially, what are we doing when we begin to pray, "Our Father . . ."?

We confess that the God who sustains this world can be trusted to sustain us. Erik Erikson says that the first requirement for human maturity is the *basic trust* learned by babies with good parents.[24] There is much in this world not worthy of human trust, and only a fool grows up thinking (with Robert Browning's Pippa) that if "God's in his heaven, all's right with the world." Why the world contains so many threats to our existence—disease, accident, violence, and death itself—is no little mystery. This "bad mystery" of evil convinces many a human that any creator of this world must be evil (a view that surfaced early in the history of the church in the heretic Marcion, who wanted to eliminate the Hebrew Bible from the Christian and to sever belief in "God the Father Almighty" from the "Creator of Heaven and Earth"). Adherents of many a religion in the world are mostly concerned to avoid evil gods and evil spirits. A secular form of this religion-of-distrust can be found among people living in the slums of some urban areas of the United States. Social workers and ministers at work here tell us that young people in such communities read in their environment of the street the constant message, "Beware!" If Erikson is right, such a world is literally unliveable for human beings. Trust nothing in the world, and you will never grow up. Ghetto youth heed this truth when they form gangs of their own peers, substitute families. The human being, even biologically considered in comparison with most other species, is a notably dependent being. Woe to us if nothing in our enviroment is dependable!

There is a lot of difference, then, between having nothing to depend on and having something. Most of us have the good

fortune to be born to parents who know how to express something dependable to their children. As already noted, even
"good" parents are irregularly trustworthy, and their self-
serving tendencies are probably in perpetual competition with
devotion to their children's interests. The mystery of evil on
earth has its expression in the depths of our fallible human
parenting, too! *That* competition does not obtain in the heart
of God the Father; but even God does not demonstrate care
for us in all times and places equally. The love of God has its
locations, alongside the locations of evil in the world. We know
that we cannot expect all of reality to sustain us. God will sustain us against the ultimate onslaught of evil, however—to
anticipate a final petition of the Lord's Prayer; and this faith
has been provoked in us by all that we see in that particular
"location" of God in our world, Jesus of Nazareth. To believe
in the God and Father of Jesus is to believe in one who raised
him from the dead. The good news is the ultimate trustworthiness of the one in whom Jesus trusted. We remember that
around the cross, some cynical witnesses taunted Jesus for his
trust in the Father:

> "He trusts in God; let God deliver him now, if he desires him;
> for he said, 'I am the Son of God.' " (Matthew 27:43)

The resurrection of Jesus is God's joyful counterpoint to this
skepticism. The resurrection is not a rational answer to the
problem of evil in this world: why is the world so arranged that
a good man like Jesus gets crucified? why does a child get can-
cer and die at the age of five? why are there homes from which
love is absent? why . . . why does God seem so inscrutably to
forsake us? The modest but unswerving Christian answer to
these questions is the example and hope that come to the world
in Jesus crucified and risen: he is the *decisive* evidence for the
trustworthiness of the God of this world. If Jesus, in the midst
of his great undeserved suffering, could continue to call God
"Father" in utmost, mysterious trust, so also may we. And if,
without seeing all the evil of earth conquered, we still "see
Jesus" (Heb. 2:9), we have—with the earliest disciples—the one

bit of evidence that makes all the difference in the world. It keeps the world trustworthy enough to live in. If Jesus put "basic trust" in the one whom he called "Father," so also can we. That, at its simplest, is the beginning of Christian faith. Rightly enough, it is what we begin to say when we begin the Lord's Prayer.

We join a company of free persons, free to be human and to live humanly anywhere, in any time, under any circumstances. We have seen that in his teachings, and especially in this prayer, Jesus addressed the human anxiety that we may not *matter.* Our frantic human propensity for proving our self-importance, for "putting on airs," and for asserting our superiority to our neighbors, is sourced in this anxiety. If we did not continue to harbor doubts about our importance as individual persons, why would we go on trying to prove it? Jesus called his disciples to enjoy their already-demonstrated value to the Father. Liberated by this confidence, they could "love [their neighbors] as [ones] like [themselves]" (Martin Buber's interpretive addition to the second great commandment).[25] They could proceed to perform works of love for neighbors, freed of the burdens of pride and anxiety about their own importance.

Jesus exhibits this freedom perpetually in his life and very death. He frequently does so in some explicit connection with his utterance of the word "Father." Go through any of the four Gospels (a concordance will help such a search), and you find him speaking the word as he prays privately, prays publicly, heals the sick, instructs the disciples, tests their theology, describes the destiny of little children, informs the disciples of their equality in God's sight, anticipates the final judgment of the world, serves the Last Supper, prays in Gethsemane, counsels against violence, dies on the cross, talks with the disciples after the resurrection, and commissions them for their ministry in the world.[26] If the bond of tender supremacy held fast for Jesus on all these occasions, on what occasion might it not hold for a disciple? You can be Paul in jail at Philippi, and still you can pray "Our Father ..." (Acts 16:25). You can be Mother

Theresa in the slums of Calcutta, and still you can pray "Our Father. . . ." You can be an astronaut on your way to the planets; a stranger in Times Square; an exile without a passport; or a young man, like Thomas Wolfe's George Webber, standing at the grave of your last human relative, and you need *not* be overwhelmed by the despair which he experienced at that graveside:

> He thought of the future opening blankly before him, and for a moment he had an acute sense of terror and despair like that of a lost child, for he felt now that the last tie that had bound him to his native earth was severed, and he saw himself as a creature homeless, uprooted and alone, with no door to enter, no place to call his own in all the vast desolation of the planet.[27]

Not so, those who can say with the psalmist:

> Cast me not off, forsake me not,
>   O God of my salvation!
> For my father and my mother have forsaken me,
>   but the LORD will take me up. (Psalm 27:9–10)

You have a new permanent identity as a human person. You are a child of God in God's own hand, and nothing can take you away from God or from yourself. "Who shall separate us from the love of Christ? Shall tribulation, or distress, or persecution, or famine, or nakedness, or peril, or sword? . . . No, in all these things we are more than conquerors through him who loved us" (Rom. 8:35, 37).

We are free to be neighbors to all the children of God. In his essay, "An Interpretation of the Debate Among Black Theologians," James Cone states that "to be Christian and human means developing a perspective on life that includes all peoples." His own work as founder of the Black Theology movement in this country has focused on the contribution of the experience of Black Americans to a contemporary understanding of God. Those people who, like the descendants of seventeenth-century slaves, experience American society from its very bottom rung, have a profoundly biblical contribution to make to that understanding. If you are a Black person in

America, says Cone, you can know something about the God of Moses and the God of Jesus that few other groups in America can know. But Black Theology is not thereby a sectarian gospel or anthropology, says he. There is "a universality implied in the particularity of Black religion," from which the whole Christian movement may learn as we engage together in "the search for a truth that defines us all."[28]

Provincialism in defining the fully human tempts all human minds and cultures, as the history of the church itself amply suggests. When was there a time in church history when its leaders were not in captivity to someone's sense of "Christian" superiority over someone else? From Paul's struggle to persuade his friend Philemon to welcome his escaped slave Onesimus back "no longer as a slave but ... as a beloved brother," to Martin Luther's proclamation of the priesthood of all believers to John Woolman's biblical arguments with slave-owners, to the current political struggle in the United States over the citizenship privileges of blacks and women and Asian immigrants, the transformation of provincial to worldwide definition of humanity goes on. Inside and outside the church, we may believe, the Holy Spirit participates in this transformation, which may remain incomplete to our history's end but will never cease to be a mighty dynamic of the coming kingdom of God. When they say "Our Father," Christians are participating in this dynamic, in that movement of the Spirit who "doesn't love a wall," who means to break open the barriers between humans across the earth.[29]

In the Lord's Prayer, Christians proclaim an open-door policy towards all human beings in the world. This is not "secular humanism" but Christian humanism, rooted squarely in the New Testament church's experience of the Holy Spirit's restless refusal to be the captive of church meeting houses (see Acts 10—11). God is the Creator and Caretaker of all the world, the Parent of all humanity. Therefore the prayer of Christians, at its most authentic, is least sectarian: there is no human on earth who is not welcomed into the great family of God. Whether all members of that family acknowledge this faith or join churches, the prayer of the churches is world-spanning and world-welcoming. As Walter Luthi puts it beautifully:

> All over the world, in America, in Russia, in the remotest parts of Turkey and Japan, and in Germany, too, there lives a host of brothers [and sisters] in faith whose numbers are known to God alone and who say the Lord's Prayer with you. They say it in different languages, it is true: but they all pray through the one Christ and to the one God in the one Holy Spirit. But the love of God does not want to stop half way, which it would be doing if it were to confine itself to the circle of believers; no, God wants to extend His [Fatherhood] to the very ends of the earth. The love of God does not let itself be limited to the community of the believing. . . . Believers cannot exclude other people when they say the Lord's Prayer: on the contrary, they include everything that bears a human face and their prayer embraces the whole of Creation. Thus the Lord's Prayer is the true and noblest prayer of intercession. Although the community prays within its own circle, it embraces all . . . and all Creation when it says, *"Our Father."*[30]

Christians are a people who have stepped through a door into a new home which is the family dwelling-place of the whole human race. They pass into that new ecumenical home in the word, *abba*. They are tasting a liberation meant for the world. They remind themselves and the world about the meaning of that liberation in their first word of prayer as taught them by Jesus. But there are other words that illumine the nature of that liberation, and to those we now turn.

CHAPTER 2

Food, Freedom, and Human Destiny

In July 1978, a group of church leaders from the United States visited eastern Europe and the U.S.S.R. During their visit to East Berlin they were invited by the Deputy Secretary of the Office of Religious Affairs of the German Democratic Republic to a breakfast at the City Hall. The Deputy Secretrary of course is a Communist. At breakfast he made this remarkable statement:

> "As Marxist-Leninists in a socialist society, building the communist society of the future in which we believe churches will disappear, we recognize that Christians and churches are a fact of life today. Indeed, citizens who are Christians are an important part of the productive force which is developing our nation, and the churches are helping in building our socialist society. This support is why we consider it normal to allocate some State funds for this support of theological chairs and institutions in our universities: church people have helped create these funds by their labor in State enterprises. You know, while Communists are certain that religion and churches are not forever, nobody knows how long there will in fact be Christians and churches in our midst. As long as there are, they are guaranteed by our Constitution equal treatment under the law, and freedom in their worship activities."

One of the American church visitors reports that the Protestant and Catholic Christians of East Germany are hard at work "resisting every State pressure that might hasten their prescribed demise. With prudence, they even try to contribute to public thinking on public issues. For example (in a recent pastoral letter), they opposed the introduction of basic military theory into the high school curriculum. . . . Such leaders expect no miraculous deliverance from dictatorship . . . but are committed to a centimeter-by-centimeter struggle for the full freedom of church witness and service, and for the promotion of the whole nation's civil liberties and rights."[1]

Many American Christians will have trouble detecting the church history that shapes the above statements. What many call "Communist East Germany" is traditionally the center of German Protestantism, the area where the Lutheran Reformation began. For the past four hundred years the churches here have related to the state in the "territorial church" tradition, a form of the medieval connection of church and government wherein government pays the salaries of clergy, supports the church's school system, and pays professors of theology in universities. The American notion of "separation of church and state" has been foreign to church-state relations in Germany for over a thousand years. In the East Berlin official's statement one can see the attempt of an avowed "post-Christian" government to cope with the institutional impact of the church and the state upon each other in this political culture. Much of that impact has been bad as the Marxists read history. For them, religion has been the "opiate of peoples," the tool of oppression of the poor by the powerful. In the Middle Ages the church blessed the feudal system with its division of society between the three "estates" of nobility, clergy, and serfs. By so blessing this system, official Christianity promoted the permanent access of a few people to power and wealth alongside a majority of the population assigned to subservience and poverty. The long-range plan of Communist government, insofar as it heeds Marxist social theories, assumes that "religion and churches are not forever." An orthodox Marxist desires to bring about the "forever" of *social justice*, the just distribution of earth's resources among all human beings. In this view the hope of humanity is access to material good, the foundation of all other human fulfillment. Marxist humanism has room in it for a richer version of human fulfillment than one consisting in a full stomach, a warm house, and a job; but it scoffs at any understanding of the richly human life which does not begin with these material preconditions. It reserves its peculiar contempt for any religion that diverts human attention from the needs of the body to the alleged needs of the soul. Such a religion is a drug that numbs the mind to social reality.

We misread church history if we deny all truth to this Marxist criticism of the church's collaboration in various injustices foisted upon poor people over the two thousand years of world history since the time of Jesus. We have already noted that the first persons to pray the Lord's Prayer were mostly poor, powerless folk. Most of them fitted Marx's definition of "proletarian." In a long series of historical social changes, however, the first-century's church-of-the-poor was to become the church-of-all-citizens (under the emperors Constantine and Justinian), the church of "Christian civilization" (in medieval Europe), the territorial church of the Lutheran Reformation, and even the church of "Christian America"—a favorite phrase among late nineteenth-century American Protestants which can be heard today on the lips of more than one television-evangelist.[2] In all these centuries we see a religion, which traces its origin to Jesus of Nazareth and which began as a minor sect, acquiring power, prestige, and wealth. During most of these centuries it was no scandal to call oneself a Christian. It was often a requirement of respectability.

In the late twentieth century, in many parts of the human world, it is no longer necessarily so. In East Germany, in increasingly secular America, and in many non-western societies, cultural prestige and power for the Christian movement is episodic. We hear Communist officials commit themselves to the fiscal support of churches, and we observe them (as in contemporary Poland) giving grudging recognition to the actual political influence of the church. But we see the irony of these concessions on their part. We know that, according to their basic secularist theory of human well-being, there really is no permanent place for the worship of God, or a church existing apart from the rest of society, or an interpretation of the world as "the theater of God's glory," as Calvin used to say.

On these latter points, practicing Christians throughout the world, if they know their faith and their Marxist critics, will indeed commit themselves to "a centimeter-by-centimeter strug-

gle for the full freedom of church witness" in their respective
societies. The present chapter of this study of the Lord's Prayer
is much concerned with this struggle, ancient and modern. But
one will misread these pages, too, not to speak of church history, if one sees here a discussion molded to the motto "Christ
versus Marx" or "Christianity against secularism." Such simplic-
ity lurks along the path of contemporary Christians as a spirit-
ual-intellectual temptation. To fall victim to that temptation is
to miss a perennial question of Christian theology and ethics
that has arisen in every era of church history: how does the
"kingdom of God" relate to all human kingdoms? How does the
Christian's loyalty to the Lord of the church affect his or her
relation to human powers, social systems, and cultures? How
does one pray, "Thy kingdom come, Thy will be done, On earth
as it is in heaven," in the midst of competing human claims to
our loyalty? The question is old and perpetual in the Christian
movement. It faces Christians in every country, time, and cir-
cumstance, calling for much personal reflection, consultation
with one's fellow Christians, and struggle in society at large.
Supremely, it calls for some basic theological, biblical orienta-
tion or standpoint for all who ask it seriously. And it calls for
scrupulous honesty about possible contrasts between this biblical-theological ground, on which Christians should stand, and
all the other grounds on which they walk in company with
human neighbors of many different cultural loyalties. Christians share many of those loyalties—"values." What does the
praying of the Lord's Prayer have to do with arranging,
assigning relative authority and worth, to those loyalties?[3]

For a start, biblical honesty will compel many modern Christians to admit that concern for the bodily needs of poor people
was no invention of Karl Marx. Such concern is as old as Moses
and Amos, and it is central to the teachings of Jesus. Here,
uncomfortably enough, a little recollection of the ensuing two
thousand years of church history—with its amassing of political,
economic, and cultural power by the church—will afflict any
faithful reader of Luke 6:20–26 with a sense of irony and perhaps repentance:

And he lifted up his eyes on his disciples, and said:
"Blessed are you poor, for yours is the kingdom of God.
Blessed are you that hunger now, for you shall be satisfied.
Blessed are you that weep now, for you shall laugh.
Blessed are you when men hate you, and when they exclude you
and revile you, and cast out your name as evil, on account of the
Son of man! Rejoice in that day and leap for joy, for behold,
your reward is great in heaven; for so their fathers did to the
prophets.
But woe to you that are rich, for you have received your
consolation.
Woe to you that are full now, for you shall hunger.
Woe to you that laugh now, for you shall mourn and weep.
Woe to you, when all men speak well of you, for so their fathers
did to the false prophets."

This human history, according to Jesus and the prophets before
him, is heavy with God's purpose to rescue the weak and the
poor from their weakness and poverty. It is equally heavy with
God's judgment upon the rich and secure. To these first hearers of his teachings, surely, these words came as good news!
Such news was more "radical"—in the "root" sense of that
word—than that of any recent western ideology. Its source was
the Maker and Finisher of the universe, the Father of all being
and all people, who hastens to end the suffering of the poor "in
a time that is drawing near."[4]

What would it mean to pray for the coming of *this* kingdom
as the end of the twentieth century draws near?

The Times and the End-time: A Biblical-theological Problem

Before venturing some direct answers to that great question,
we have reason to return to the text and context of the Lord's
Prayer with a preliminary question that has perplexed theologians, especially recent students of the prayer. The perplexity
grows out of the tone of urgency, crisis, and imminent change
in passages like Luke 6, the language of the Lord's Prayer, and
the New Testament as a whole. A cursory reading of all twenty-
seven books of the New Testament will convince anyone that
the early Christian church spoke and lived with intense expectation of the coming *end* of human history. In the crucifixion and

resurrection of Jesus, the early church saw the oncoming of God's final battles with evil on earth. No one, Jesus has warned (not even he)[5] knew just when God's ending of history would come. But an end there would be, a judgment, a setting-right of all the wrong that afflicts human history down to the end.

The word that summarizes this context is "eschatological" (after the Greek word *eschaton*, the end). The Lord's Prayer, as some scholars now read it, was originally an intensely eschatological prayer, full of yearning for the coming climax of God's rule on earth, the final breaking-in of the "kingdom that has been ready for you since the world was made" (Matt. 25:34). And, said Jesus, "this generation will not pass away till all these things take place" (Matt. 24:34).

For anyone like myself, interested in the "social ethics of the Lord's Prayer," this perspective poses a problem. I am far from the first to have the problem. It surfaced in the early church before the end of the first century. By then, *seventy* years had passed since the resurrection—three whole human generations—and the end of the world had not yet come! Might the church have to adjust to an indefinite delay in the end-time? Indeed, adjust it did: it devised an international church organization bound together by bishops; it arranged a system of instruction for the children of believers, generation to generation; it compiled some instructions for daily Christian living in a pagan world; it collected an authoritative set of writings, embodying the heart of the early church's message, that would become our New Testament; and it composed several brief formal creeds for instructing new converts and for drawing the line against heretics. All these measures expressed the growing necessity and will of the church to settle down and to live indefinitely with the ongoing particularities of human culture, economics, and politics. Very gradually, over many future centuries, the church thus moved away from its expectation of the imminent end of history towards a sense of the permanency and stability in its relation to the whole of ordinary human life in society. From time to time, various voices arose to call the church's attention to the original eschatological expectation of the New Testament church. A number of these radicals were sure that the end would come exactly in the year A.D. 1000. But by then the majority of church people were inclined to label these voices as fanatic; and, besides, the year 1000 passed without the world's coming to its end. The majority-minority views among the earliest Christians were probably reversed. Back in A.D. 50, as Paul was writing his letters to the church in Corinth, the Apostle was so sure of the short time left the human race and all its "kingdoms" that he could dismiss the contemporary world of culture and its institutions as "a wisdom belonging to this passing age (and) . . . its governing powers, which are declining to their end" (1 Cor. 2:6, NEB). Like all human organizations, the Roman Empire did "decline to its end." But that took four hundred years, and by then even Christians had become so used to the social security of that empire that Augustine wrote his book, *The City of God*, partly to reassure them that the kingdom of God could survive the decline and fall of any empire! The church by then was already taking account of its relation to government and other social realities. Paul could bypass most of this in his eager expectation of "the splendour . . . which is in store for us" (Rom. 8:18, NEB). The church in history could not bypass it.

What does this mean for us who now pray the Lord's Prayer almost two thousand years after Jesus first uttered it? Should we simply ignore the eschatological sense of this prayer? Are we, too, compelled to settle down in history; to abandon the early Christian memory of Jesus' words, "The kingdom of God is at hand" (Mark 1:15); and to treat, as one more myth, the notion that our history has an end-purpose and an end-time? Some contemporary fundamentalists, spiritually akin to some of Augustine's fearful contemporaries, are sure that the threatened collapse of global human society under the devastation of a nuclear war constitutes the near approach of the divine doomsday, any moment now, in the twentieth century. God will soon wind things up—with nuclear missiles. These modern apocalypticists are victims of a superficial reading of the New Testament. It is not within human power, Jesus says clearly and repeatedly, for war and rumor of war to bring about *God's* ending of the human story. Nuclear holocaust—like every other crime against humanity—may indeed be heavy with divine judgment upon our collective sins. But the end foreseen by Jesus was as heavy with blessing as with judgment for the human race, its "nations," and its individual persons (cf. Matt. 25:31–46).

Again, Jesus is clearly ignorant about the timing of it all: "Of that day and hour no one knows, not even the angels of heaven, nor the Son, but the Father only" (Matt. 24:36). In short, *Christians will always have to deal with some "meantime."* Faithful Christian prayer will continue to root in the confidence that God really is "working his purpose out, as year succeeds to year," as history moves towards the great consummation when at last

> . . . the earth shall be filled with the glory of God
> As the waters cover the sea.[6]

Christian discipleship is life between the times: this is the basic truth which new scholarship underlines for us in our attempt here to frame a social ethic appropriate to praying the Lord's Prayer. Yearnings for the final divine transformation of earth and of our daily existence both belong to this prayer. Very soon both combined in the early church's use of the prayer. Raymond E. Brown summarizes this development as follows:

> Already in the Lucan form of the (Lord's Prayer) . . . the intensity of eschatological aspiration has begun to yield to the hard facts of daily Christian living. It is a sign of the genius of this prayer, taught by the divine Master, that it could serve to express such different aspirations. Nevertheless, as we say the prayer nineteen centuries later, now completely enmeshed in the temporal aspect of the Christian life, it would, perhaps, profit us to revive in part some of its original eschatological yearning.[7]

When the Lucan version of the prayer (11:1–4) speaks of "daily bread," for example, Luke's account of Jesus' blessing of the hungry and needy (6:20–26) leaps readily to mind. It is hard to believe that in the early church hungry people could have

prayed fervently for bread at the great end-time banquet without thinking also of their need for bread *now*. Nowhere in his
teaching does Jesus grant an opening to some future materialist
philosopher to accuse him of postponing the divine fulfillment
of human need to "by and by." Nor is God's rule, now or then,
only a spiritual rule in the individual hearts of believers. As Professor Brown puts it, when the Christian community prays "Thy
kingdom come,"

> it is identifying with the divine plan. The Christians are not pri-
> marily asking that God's dominion come into their own hearts
> . . . but that God's universal reign be established—that destiny
> toward which the whole of time is directed.

> In Jesus' preaching there is virtually no emphasis on the next
> life as distinct from the final coming of God's kingdom.[8]

At the beginning of this book I confessed that as a culture
we moderns are not very skillful at "relating things." Nor do we
find it easy to live, as Dietrich Bonhoeffer believed we must live,
in "many different dimensions" at once.[9] When we get up in the
morning, we may have the spiritual discipline to pray for the
fulfillment of the ultimate purposes of God in human history,
but we turn quickly to our work of the day and get quite
drowned in the pursuit of our own immediate purposes. The
grace of Christian discipleship—the power of the Spirit-led
life—surely consists of a connecting of these two dimensions.
The necessity of this connection confronts us powerfully in the
most extensive series of teachings about the end-time to be
found in the Gospel writings—Matthew 24 and 25. These chapters are full of Jesus' anticipation of God's final triumph over
the kingdoms of the human world. But at the final judgment,
he says, many humans will be surprised at how seriously, all
along, the Father of all humans was concerned with the daily
needs of creatures and their obligations to serve each other in
the meeting of these needs. Fail to feed, clothe, house, comfort,
and visit your needy neighbor on earth, and you will fail God's
final examination of your part in human history (Matt.

25:31–36)! Here is a kind of "dialectical materialism" quite different from the one that Marxists describe: the interaction that God intends humans to have between the good they do today and the good they hope God will do "on earth as it is in heaven." God does not exempt even himself from that interaction for the good news is that in Jesus of Nazareth God participated in human neediness, establishing for all time the most urgent conceivable reason for taking politics, economics, and social justice seriously: "For I was hungry and you gave me food . . . " (Matt. 25:35).

How then do we solve the problem of time-focus in our praying of the Lord's Prayer? As many faithful Christians have solved it: we forget neither the "now" nor the "then" of God's will for earth, neither the short nor the long of it. We go about today's tasks in the faith that they too are important for God's purposes. This very moment is a moment *of* eternity. Each bit of true obedience to the will of God is a thread in the tapestry of the Great Weaver. We do not forget that this divine plan is far more wonderful "than all that we ask or think" (Eph. 3:20) in any moment of our lives. But we do not thereby neglect the things we can ask or think.

Martin Luther caught the essence of this double focus, and the humility of Christian discipleship, when someone asked him: "What would you do if you knew that the end of the world was coming tomorrow?" "I would go out and plant a tree," replied Luther.

We cannot truly know when the end will come. We cannot know all that God intends to do in time or at the end of time, to establish the great kingdom. But we know enough to live in the meantime. And we know by what standard our part in it all will be judged worthy or wanting when that end comes.[10]

In Two Dimensions: Food and Freedom

So to interpret the time-sense of the Lord's Prayer is to believe that Christians in every age must learn to pray the prayer in relation to that age as well as to the age to come. Fidelity to the divine Ruler of history requires openness to signs of that rule right before our eyes as each age of world history experiences some new glimmer of that kingdom-to-come. When Christians pray "Thy kingdom come, Thy will be done," they know the fear and trembling of their own opportunities to frustrate or to serve that kingdom and that will. There are votes to be cast, causes for which to be sacrificed, neighbors waiting outside our doors in need, all testing now whether we believe in a kingdom of real justice on earth or in some disembodied ideal or illusion. We are come, like Esther, to this particular place "for such a time as this" (Esther 4:14). Remembering the Lord Jesus and many centuries when other Christians made their faithful witness, we too "wait in confidence and joy for our deliverance," but in the meantime we "give ourselves to those tasks which lie to our hands and so set up signs that men may see."[11]

Someone has said that the faith of Christians requires them to keep the Bible in one hand and the daily newspaper in the other. If the one informs us of a divine self-revelation still seeking us, the other informs us of the realm in which that revelation now encounters us. If the one informs us of a hope and purpose that transcends any news-of-the-day, the other reminds us that we have our own daily news to make in view of a purpose towards which all creation moves.

As the opening illustration of this chapter suggests, this double-alertness of the Christian to the biblical and the contemporary perspectives is likely to confront us with two large dimensions of contemporary political-economic life. Let us tag these two "food and freedom." Let us then ask how the early church wrestled with the relation between these two. Then, finally, let us circle back to the question of how Christians in East Germany and the United States ought to pray "Thy kingdom come" *and* "Give us this day our daily bread."

Fundamental Freedom: The New Testament Church at Worship

As part of their corporate worship, the Lord's Prayer has been uttered most often among Christians on "the Lord's Day"—Sunday, the first day of the week in the western calendar. Why did that day "belong" to Jesus? Because on that day,

the apostles remembered he rose from the dead: on that convic-
tion the early church staked its faith, life, and weekly day of
worship.

No one can "prove" the resurrection of Jesus, but an arrest-
ing set of reasons for taking that belief seriously clusters, in the
New Testament, around the very existence of the church as a
social organization soon after the crucifixion of Jesus. We read
in Acts that the official leaders of religion and government
"began to wonder" at the "boldness of Peter and John" (4:13)
and other members of the young church. Once, in the terrible
hours just before Jesus' execution, Peter had cowered before
these same leaders. Now, a few weeks afterwards, here he was
with other disciples, fearlessly engaged in a public meeting in
the name of Jesus. Apparently this public group of witnessing
Christians had "come from nowhere," just as Jesus had
returned from the dead out of the nowhereness of death. Like
Israel brought up from Egypt, like the world created from
nothing, the church came into history as a surprise. In this context, one can say that the living church has always been a proof
that Jesus really is risen.

There is an ethical claim hidden in this claim of faith. Scholars have long asked if a "social ethic" can be found in the New
Testament, i.e., a set of guidelines for Christian behavior in a
secular society. Their answer has been: "A very partial set of
guidelines at most." Search from Matthew to Revelation, and
you will find little systematic guidance on the best way to organize economic production and distribution, or how to structure a
government to eliminate class privilege or racial discrimination.
The New Testament does not even have a consistent view of
slavery, an institution whose cruelties affected many Christians
of the time. Centuries would pass before the church developed
clear ethical principles on some economic and political questions, and on some others it developed hardly any principles at
all. But from the very beginning, the church's slim bundle of
ethics had at its center a certain core of steel: *it refused to
acknowledge the religious authority—the lordship—of Caesar.* That
refusal was intimately connected with the resurrection of Jesus

by which, they believed, God had declared him "whom you crucified, both Lord and Messiah" (Acts 2:36, NEB). The declaration *Kurios Jesous* ("Jesus is Lord") stood at the start of the
Christian witness like the preamble to a developing, incomplete
political constitution. It was one principle of social ethics on
which they would unite for the next three centuries until a
Roman emperor finally acceded to the point. During these
three centuries, along with the Jews, Christians regularly antag-
onized Roman officials by their refusal to worship the emperor
alongside the God of Moses, the Father of the Lord Jesus. Early
Christians were not revolutionaries, and they largely accepted
the power of Rome as legitimate government.[12] But they
refused to apply for a license from Rome to practice their religion, for they knew that the license was granted on the condition that practitioners of this or that religion would attend to
their annual burning of incense before the altar to Caesar in
every local town square of the empire. "You may worship any
way you like," said the tolerant Roman policy, "if you will salute
our emperor and acknowledge his supreme authority in the
realm of politics. Give him the monopoly in practical governmental affairs, and we will not interfere with your private
religion."

It seemed a modest request to most Romans, even to those
who were inwardly skeptical about the emperor's politic claim to
divinity. But Christians and Jews would not consent. The
Romans tried every pressure to get them to consent. To jail, to
the gladiatorial arena, to crucifixion they went; but faithful
Christians would not shape their tongues around the words,
"Caesar is Lord." How could they do so once they had shaped
their tongues around the prayer that the real Lord had taught
them? "Hallowed be *thy* name!" As we have seen, along with
their Hebrew predecessors, the early Christians understood the
name of anything as belonging to its inmost nature. Some words
are not removable stickers; remove them, and you remove the
reality. This is supremely so of the words that name God, so
that at some point or another, language about God may be a
matter of fidelity or idolatry. The Roman magistrates caught on

to this way of thinking enough to know how to detect it in their judicial procedures; anyone accused of being a Christian was asked to repeat out loud the formula of political obedience, *Kurios Caesar*. "No," said the faithful, "it just is not so. It is a lie: Jesus is Lord, and of that we have been assured in that he rose from the death a deputy of the emperor imposed upon him. The world is not *really* organized around Caesar. It is organized about God its Creator and our Father, who is revealed in Jesus and present with us in the Holy Spirit. Government too is a creature of this King of the universe. Though we respect human government, we will not worship it. Before we will do so, we will die with the Lord's Prayer on our lips."

One could speak of the Lord's Prayer, and especially its opening section, therefore, as the ground of the early church's resistance to politicized idolatry. As such, Christian prayer has always resisted what today we call totalitarianism. In no modern sense was ancient Rome totalitarian, but its leaders understood well one secret to tight central control of public order: keep the "private" beliefs of individuals effectively segregated from "public" activity; and do so by keeping close watch over all *group* meetings, even the smallest. Who could be sure what rebellions might be discussed in such "unlicensed" gatherings—like volunteer fire departments and Christian worship services?[13]

The stubborn insistence of Christians on ascribing Lordship to Jesus alone continued until A.D. 312, when Constantine came to the conclusion that the Christians had the most vigorous religion in the empire. (Historians estimate that perhaps ten percent of the population of the empire had become professing Christians by the early fourth century.) Constantine's realism was quite similar to that of the Communist Deputy Secretary in East Berlin. Communist governments around the world today are dealing circumspectly with the claim of the churches to freedom of worship. Down through history, the more a government has denied such freedom, the more stubborn some Christians have become. They go underground for their worship. They go to jail and continue praying there. They become a political problem no matter what you do to them. "So why not let them be at least for a while? They have a slogan, 'The blood of the martyrs is the seed of the church.' If you want eventually to kill the church, why not let it live for now?" From Roman provincial governors to the police chiefs of modern dictatorships, it has seemed the shrewdest, most practical strategy!

Here is the irony: that some secularists and many Christians should agree on the same basic political point: *a society should permit freedom of worship.* This is a first contribution that Christians (along with some other religious movements and some agnostics like Voltaire who personally preferred no religion at all) have made to the political culture of the world.

The theological roots of this contribution, on the Christian side, lie exposed in the second petition of the Lord's Prayer: "Thy kingdom come, Thy will be done, On earth as it is in heaven." As we distinguish between human parenthood and divine parenthood when we call God "Our Father," so when we speak of God's kingdom we distinguish it from our human kingdoms. These phrases spell death for idolatry in all its forms, including its governmental and churchly forms. God did not banish Caesar from his divine status in order to raise a bishop or a pope or a General Assembly to the same! All the empires and all the churches of history do not equal the kingdom of God.

The liberation of humanity here is twofold. On the one hand, humans are not destined by God to be the slaves of political, ecclesiastical, economic, or other institutional powers. The church that gathers for worship testifies to this freedom from the ultimate subjection of any of us to any of the rest of us. But there is another side to the liberation: we are free now to be a people of God and not just a collection of individuals. The same liturgical act that acclaims the priority of the kingdom of God in the world embodies that claim *socially.* Christian worship is the act of a community. In that community we are not only freed from the powers of this world; we are simultaneously freed to care for our neighbor in the world. In chapter one we underscored the inescapable social nature of the Lord's Prayer and its equally inescapable human universality. A Christian congrega-

tion, on any Sunday morning anyplace on earth, is a doorway to
that universality. As such, a church at worship is free from ultimate subservience to provincialism. Whatever may be the right
relation between Christian discipleship and local cultural loyalties, the Lord's Prayer acclaims the priority of the one over the
other. We are free from subservience to some of our neighbors
to become serviceable to them all. We are free to be human
before we are free to be, for example, American. This is one
reason why the notion of "Christian America" should provoke
American Christians to a sense of ambiguity and suspicion.
Even if every citizen of the United States were a church member, ambiguity and suspicion would have to remain—as with the
notions "Christian Europe" and "Holy Roman Empire."

No nation, government, or culture on earth deserves the
unrestrained, unconditional respect of Christians; for membership in a particular cultural or political community is not the
first fact of our life. The first fact is our solidarity with human
beings everywhere. As we pray our Lord's Prayer, we know that
our American neighbor has no higher value in the kingdom of
God than our neighbor in India and Zimbabwe. *Human solidarity
over provincial solidarity:* that is the universalistic rule for those
who wish to pray the prayer of the Lord in its spirit and truth.
In obedience to that rule lies a great liberty, "the glorious liberty
of the children of God" (Rom. 8:21). As first fruit of that liberty, in historic societies this side of the end-time, the church
lays claim to social freedom to engage in its collective worship.

Bread for the World, the Other Freedom

Interpreted against the background of both church history
and the social history of humanity as a whole, the Lord's Prayer
may prompt in some of us the sober question: *is it possible to build
a society that is both "free" and "just"?*

In our own day this question grows out of the apparent conflict between the proponents of "liberal democracy" and "social
democracy." The liberals (along with Thomas Jefferson) put a
high priority on the obligation of government to promote and
protect its people's enjoyment of certain personal and group

rights. The socialists (along with Karl Marx) put a similar high priority on government's obligation to promote and protect its people's enjoyment of equal access to resources for meeting their economic and social needs. On the one side, proponents say, "If we have to choose between liberty and justice, we choose liberty!" And the others say, "We choose justice!"

Raised as we are in a liberal-democratic society, many Americans have little difficulty siding with the first answer. Our society has apparently provided the majority of Americans with both food and freedom in abundance. We would be more understanding neighbors to our neighbors in various parts of earth, however, if we appreciated their reasons for siding with the second answer. The American journalist Hedrick Smith acquired some such appreciation in his numerous conversations with people in the Soviet Union in the early nineteen-seventies. Many Soviets, he concluded, really do "prefer their socialism to the freer but less secure life style of Westerners. . . . For many, the benefits of low-cost housing, free medical care, subsidized university education, and a guaranteed job—above all, that job security—outweigh the disadvantages of the marketplace" and other freedoms of the west. As one Russian said to Smith: "I have a specialty. I can walk out of my institute and get another job in my specialty and I will make the same money, 220 rubles a month, without any problem. I can count on my 220 rubles. That is the big difference. I don't have to worry about the future, and you do!"[14]

In a time of high unemployment in the United States and unemployment rates in the Third World like Mexico's forty percent, much human peril and pain surround the great social question: must a society choose between food and freedom? The Lord's Prayer has no simple contribution to make to the modern ideological quarrels that seethe around this question; but as we cross the bridge from "Thy will be done" to "Give us this day our daily bread," we do well to suspect that, in the kingdom of God an either/or choice will be abolished. In all earthly institutional anticipations of that kingdom, it must be abolished in some measure. God's destiny for us humans requires our

freedom and our food. If one political implication of the first
section of the Lord's Prayer is the freedom of the worshiping
church from subservience to human governments, one economic implication of the second part is the freedom of us all
from physical want. When William Temple called Christianity
"the most avowedly materialistic of the great religions,"[15] he
had New Testament teaching in mind like the Lord's Prayer
and Matthew 25: 31–46 and John 1:l4—"the word became
flesh." On the basis of these passages alone, Walter Luthi is justified in saying that in Jesus "the social problem, the problem of
food, has become God's problem."[16]

"For *I* was hungry and you gave *me* food" (Matt. 25:35). This
astounding assertion—that the Creator of us all silently pleads
in every human for neighborly help—forms the basis of the
Christian's inescapable negotiations with the blessings and the
curses of human economic systems. It also impels us to participate, again, in that peculiar stretching discipline of living
between the "now" of daily human need and the "then" of
God's final triumph over wrong in the world. One symbol of
that triumph, in the New Testament, is the heavenly *banquet*.
Jesus brought the spiritual and material dimensions of a fully
human life together in just this symbol, in the occasion we call
his Last Supper. There, bread became the sign of God's presence in the human world, the promise of that presence through
much suffering to come, and the triumph of the kingdom at the
end of time. "As my Father appointed a kingdom for me, so I
appoint you to eat and drink at my table in the kingdom" (Luke
22:29–30).

The simplest principle in this discipline is that Christians
who yearn to sit at the Lord's table, either on some Sunday
morning in a church or at the heavenly banquet of God's final
victory-celebration, had better busy themselves in securing ordinary bread for their neighbors. No expectation of the world's
end, no "rapture," must take the disciple's mind off that rule
for obedience-in-the-meantime.[17]

It is worth noting that, in choosing the word "bread" (or
"food") to signify the bodily nourishment we all need for sur-

vival on earth, Jesus spoke as a person born after the agricultural revolution. Agriculture began three to four thousand years prior to his birth, probably in the same region of the world. Prior to this new technology, humans gathered food from forests, hunted it down, or raised it by domesticating animals. Eventually in some rich-soiled regions, alongside rivers, they learned to save and to sow the seeds of edible plants. They harvested grain, learned how to pound it into flour, and invented bread.

Here, implicitly, is a superb instance of Jesus' faith in God as both Lord of nature and Lord of human society. Jesus bids his disciples to trust God to sustain the earth that sustains good crops. More: the prayer does not ask only for rain and soil fertility; it asks for bread, a product of human labor.

> Be present, Father, where bread is baked and where its price is set until finally we see it on our tables! Be present in the kitchens of the world, so that the cooks who put flour and water together to make ricecake, *chapati*, or wheat bread will know that they are the last precious links between the will of God in heaven and the will of God for earth! Camp in the midst of our manufacturing systems that make bread, our distribution systems that make it available, our wage systems that enable us to buy it, and our governmental systems that can enable the money-less not to starve!

Even today in the United States, some Christians argue that feeding hungry people is one thing, but taking sides in arguments over economic systems is quite another. Surely the Lord's Prayer does not commit us as Christians to either capitalism or socialism, but it does commit us to testing every economic system by whether or not it does in fact alleviate or contribute to human hunger. Americans share a common intellectual-spiritual temptation here. We are a rich country, many of us are overfed, and the vast majority of us have had little vivid experience of a whole day of real hunger. We probably would encounter less political resistance to a Federal Food Stamp Program if more Americans could remember such a day in their lives. During World War II military researchers conducted experiments on the effects of hunger on people, and they found that among the hungry, food becomes the only topic of conversation. Interest in food eclipses interest in sex. It drives the individual in the direction of extreme self-preoccupation. The "natural" prayer of the hungry person, or a person that fears hunger, would be, "Lord, give me this day my daily bread, and don't take away my bread to feed someone else."

A devastating, inadvertant experiment along these same lines occurred in East Africa some few years ago in a tribe called the Ik. Colin Turnbull, an anthropologist, has recorded the grim story in his book, *The Mountain People*.[18] For many centuries, the Ik had been a hunting people, but the government of Uganda decided to move the tribe from its traditional homeland to an area where it would have to learn agriculture. The transition was too sudden for them, and gradually their ability to find food for themselves deteriorated. Whole families began to starve. The tribal bond began to break. In the extremity of their own hunger, younger people hoarded food to keep it away from the elderly. Mothers even refused food to their children. An Ik child of three years shifted for him or herself as a food-gatherer. Before they began to recover some measure of their ability to cooperate with each other, the Ik descended to the form of society described pessimistically by Thomas Hobbes: the "war of all against all," a society of utter individualists, whose contempt of each other's needs rendered the lives of all "nasty, brutish, and short."

Recent news about the Ik is encouraging: the government is helping to restore their ability to produce food. But, in the meantime, they have provided the world with macabre proof of what happens to the human community when it suffers dire hunger: it dissolves.

The truly frightening lesson of the Ik is their picture of how every one of us might behave if we become hungry enough. Their story causes me to leap ahead to the next petition or two of the Lord's Prayer with my own desperate paraphrase-of-desperation: "Give me enough daily bread, Lord, to lead me away from my temptation to fight even with my own family for food. Deliver me from the evil of my own capacity for selfishness!" (How easily prayer in the first-person singular insinuates itself here. It is one of our temptations even in our struggle against temptation. How hard, to keep praying the Lord's Prayer in its true, unremitting socialness. "Give *us* this day *our* daily bread, Father. Without bread spread around this human community we will see your name desecrated in hungry human faces and in the horrible hatreds of which we all are capable. Give us bread, that our society with one another may not suffer utter wreckage!")

There are four billion human beings living on this planet now, and over half of them suffer from some form of malnourishment. The hungry faces are there, if we dare to see them. The image of God in those faces is already being desecrated. Experts predict that by the year 2000, if present trends continue, some six hundred million persons in the world will be starving to death. Right now in thirty-five countries ("The Fourth World"), forty percent of the populace carry on a constant battle against starvation. What a spiritual burden for well-fed Christians, like the authors and readers of books like this, to remember these starving brothers and sisters as we pray the Lord's Prayer! But there is no way to pray this prayer in spirit and truth without including those starving neighbors in our focus of consciousness. And there is no way to rise from such a prayer without joining in a social struggle to rid those neighbors of their hunger—sooner, not later; now, in history, not at the heavenly banquet. If we wait until God remedies the hunger of his poor people at that great table, we shall not be there to partake of the feast.

The Church in the Struggle for Food and Freedom

Crossing the bridge between the kingdom-petition and the bread-petition, I have interpreted the Lord's Prayer as Christian hope for human society in which worship is free and bread is available to all. Few local societies measure up to this double criterion. World society as a whole falls miserably short of it. What tasks are implied for Christians, in such a world, as they pray like this?

*We must work for a society that offers religious freedom and economic
justice to all citizens—not just Christians.* The early church
claimed a freedom for its worship in defiance of some features
of the official public order. We have seen how a certain peace
with that order came with Constantine's Edict of Toleration in
A.D. 312; how it was then no longer a crime to worship Jesus as
Lord; how less than a century passed before the Roman government's traditional suspicion of unregulated religion pro-
duced the Edict of Theodosius declaring Christianity *alone* as
the permissible religion. Since these early centuries churches
have been the inconsistent friends of religious and other freedoms that modern democratic ideologies have celebrated.
Freedom of religion in the United States evolved historically
from coalitions of religious and secularist thinkers and from
the need for peace between rival sectarian groups among
Christians themselves.

One lesson of this history is that religious freedom does rest,
for its effective exercise, upon a certain public order. Christians
should read this history as full of compelling reasons to arrange
society so that freedom of worship (including the freedom not
to worship) is a right of all citizens. Another lesson is that legally
established churches are usually the enemy of such a public
order. Real toleration—"freedom for the thought we hate"[19]—
requires a certain amount of personal and institutional self-
denial. As a principle of public order, it requires religious
humility in the face of other people's religion.

Such humility was inherent in the view of Jesus and the
prophets that God's work in the world could not be limited to
the realm of formal religious organization. The pagan Assyrian
may have been the "rod" of divine anger against Israel (Isa.
10:5); the scarcely-religious, ordinary person from the "high-
ways and byways" of the community may have been a more will-
ing guest at the divine banquet than the faithful churchgoer
(Luke 14:15–24); and the Holy Spirit is capable of pioneering
wider membership for the church than its official leaders have
yet anticipated (Acts 10:1–48). Out of a true reverence for the
greatness of God, therefore, Christians will support a social

order that puts law and government on the side of religious pluralism.

This is not to say that religion itself is necessarily a "good thing" or that religious organization should be exempt from the bar of ethical judgment concerning its use of its freedoms. Going to church on Sunday is no substitute for the struggle for social justice on Monday, and woe to those who make it so (Amos 5:21–24; Matt. 5:23–24; 25:31 ff.; *et cetera ad infinitum*)! Hypocrisy lurks in the pews of those Christians who pray for "daily bread" and go home to forget about the hunger of their neighbors down the block—or over the border. If, as the Calvinists say, the chief purpose of being human is "to glorify God and to enjoy him forever," we must see bread as a tangible beginning of this enjoyment. Who can muster "joy in the Lord," on any Sunday, on an empty stomach? And what glory can there be to the Father of Jesus in hungry faces lifted in prayer? Kathe Kollwictz has a poignant drawing of a gaunt little child clawing at her mother's skirt with a desperate cry, "Bread!" The spirit of such a cry belongs here in the midst of the Lord's Prayer. To pray "thy kingdom come" and "give us bread" is to pray for a society in which all are free to praise God and all have the strength to do so.

We must support political movements and programs that call for both food and freedom. In the early 1970s, the denomination to which I belonged, undertook a program of sustained study and action on the problem of hunger in this country and the world. Few biblically literate members of this church needed to be told that Jesus commanded his followers to feed the hungry. Less traditional in the denomination had been the recognition that, under modern conditions of agriculture and commerce, bread arrives on most dinner tables of earth, if it arrives, via large economic-political systems. On the issue of bread for the world, Christians will have to give up all vestiges of the old notion that "religion and politics don't mix." In the mid-seventies, for example, at an official meeting of the General Assembly Mission Board of the Presbyterian Church, United States, someone announced that legislation was then pending in the U.S. Congress to extend or to cut back the American food-aid program for hungry peoples around the world. As the Board fell to discussing this bill in the context of the denomination's new hunger program, its members recognized the link between the two. Many of them, some for the first time in their lives, rushed to telephone their representatives in Congress, asking for support of the bill. For some upper-middle-class southern Presbyterians, it was a new thing to do.

In a society like the United States, Christians must increasingly use their political freedom to promote justice for the world's poor. Over a decade ago the British economist Barbara Ward, a Roman Catholic, called Christians of the world to see themselves as representatives of the interests of the world's poor inside their respective countries. In affluent America, the existence of any hunger among our own citizens is a national disgrace. So much more the reason, then, for a Federal Food Stamp Program. But Americans' need for bread cannot be the exclusive focus of the prayers and political struggles of American Christians. Who will represent the hungry of Uganda, Chad, India, and Bangladesh before the United States Congress, if not Christians? Who will represent the interests of the hungry outside India, before the New Delhi Parliament, if not Christians? But churches can make no such political witness if they have no freedom to make it. So, in countries like the Soviet Union and the German Democratic Republic, the churches cannot cease their struggle for that freedom, however justified these governments may be in accusing the Christian movement of collaborating with proponents of social injustice in the past. Socialist critics of capitalist societies are often correct in accusing those societies of favoring various liberties for individuals and groups over the achievement of economic justice. Liberal democratic critics of socialist societies are often correct in accusing those societies of favoring economic justice over political and religious freedom. Again, the people who pray for God's kingdom to come on earth yearn for a society which is both just and free! The priority-claims which the church must promote may be different in different societies, but the ecumenical vision is the same.

To be sure, no political party or government can be tagged by the church as permanent bearer of this vision. Two thousand years of church history and much contemporary experience support this caution. Many Christians in South India in the elections of 1957, for example, out of their yearning for economic justice for poor people, and out of disappointment in the Congress party that had ruled India for a decade, helped vote into power, in the state government of the region, a communist administration. After some years in power the Communists, too, fell victim to bribery, office-buying, and foot-dragging on programs for distributing land to landless farmers of the area. A distinguished Indian Christian, a former official of the World Bank, commented on these matters to me in response to a question which I asked him in 1978 in Bombay, "What does India need most?"

"Two things," he answered promptly. "One, a genuine land reform that will put power and economic ability into the hands of a large proportion of our village farmers. No political party yet, not even the Communists in Kerala, have effected such a reform. Two, India needs a genuinely *universal* ethic, a set of standards for our behavior as citizens applied to all of us without distinction of religion, caste, class, or economic interest. Our trouble is that we are always falling apart into our special interests without regard for the interests of the public."

It was an answer to humble an American. Indian and American politics are not all that different! Especially in countries that style themselves democratic, various special interests are free to pursue those interests in legislative halls where poor people are likely to get the short end of policy. Part of their poverty, after all, is that they are poorly organized for political purposes. Honest Christians and honest partisans of democracy will not expect particular political parties or movements to be eternally trustworthy vehicles for "liberty and justice for all." If they *are* honest, they will be suspicious of their *own* self-interest in this or that party, policy, or law. They will not cease to struggle against the natural bias of human politics towards the strong. The ethical-theological bias of the Bible is towards the

weak. Empirically considered, they are the ones most in danger
of being left in the dust of the fast-movers and the power-
grabbers. As Walter Rauschenbush put it: in most human organizations "the strong have enough power to defend their just
interests, and usually enough power left over to defend their
unjust interests too."[20] The same wisdom applies to powerful
Christians and their powerful churches.

Because we do have a prior ethical concern for justice to the
poor, and because the principle is not likely to become the
monopoly of any political party, government, or body of law, we
can make some judgments about what does and does not serve
the kingdom of God in the ways our society distributes bread to
its citizens. Food Stamp and job training programs of the government must be both welcomed and scrutinized on grounds of
this ethic. All such programs themselves are capable of corrup-
tion, as when most of the money for a national job training program or money for international food aid is siphoned off by the
middle class and the rich before it ever reaches the truly poor.
Laws and programs of government have no sanctity in themselves, and we Christians must not confuse these political con-
trivances with the coming kingdom of God. But we must relate
them to what is coming. In 1982, the White House was proposing to Congress cuts in the welfare program that approximately
equaled the cost of the new F-18 fighter plane for the U.S. Air
Force; and any overview of the administration's budget
revealed that, far from being a balanced budget, it merely
shifted funds, which in previous budgets supported various
human services, to the military side of the ledger. Any such proposal should raise some deep suspicions in the minds of American Christians in the nineteen-eighties. To be sure, there are
technical and disputable features of food policy, welfare policy,
and defense policy in the politics of any nation. But on some
points people who pray the Lord's Prayer must not be intimi-
dated by the cry, "You don't know all the facts!" We have our
own expertness with which to reply to that. Does any Bible
reader think that the Hebrew prophets and Jesus of Nazareth
would go along nimbly with a proposal to strengthen a missile

system at the cost of closing up day care centers for children of working mothers? Is the policy choice here wholly one of technicalities? *Justice for the poor is a condition of life inside a nation which makes it worth defending internationally.* Christians who adopt this biblical bedrock-principle will use it in their definitions of patriotism, national strength, and democracy. They will use it in their critique of budgets of every size and institutional location, including the budgets of churches.

Earlier in the teachings which Matthew has collected and which contain his version of the Lord's Prayer, we read of Jesus' intention that his disciples be "the salt of the earth" and "the light of the world" (Matt. 5:13–14). This hardly means that Christians have their own special wisdom for all complex political and economic problems of the world. But it does mean that we enter into political struggle equipped with certain hopes for the world and certain commitments to our neighbors around the world. We must choose our political structures carefully. We must use our freedom of worship as reminder that no government, party, or system owns us body and soul. Freed to serve God in systems where God's name is poorly hallowed or not at all, we try to "salt" and "illumine" those systems. In that political process, we ourselves may become saltier, brighter, wiser. Indeed, contemporary social research suggests that the "saltiest" Christians in America are those who trust the universal purpose of God enough to take the leap into some form of public politics—everything from letters to Congress to petitions to City Council to attendance at party precinct meetings. Justice for poor people is a cause served or misserved by public policy. If we seek a world with bread enough for all, we must involve ourselves in those public structures where the rights and interests of the whole human community are at stake. No Christian can serve a world human community in a religious spirit that thrives chiefly inside a church building. The Spirit that cries *abba* is the Spirit who hovered over the unformed creation and who now causes us to "groan inwardly while we wait for God to make us his [children] and set our whole body free" (Rom. 8:23, NEB). That Spirit hovers over the legislative halls of city, state,

national, and world political systems, too. In order to understand some things that "the Spirit says to the churches" (Rev.
2:7) in today's world, we have to listen to what is happening in
those halls. There are words of the Lord that we shall never
hear until we stand in such places, struggling with at least a few
political colleagues to persuade some majority to adopt policies
that reflect our obligation as a society "to do justice, and to love
kindness, and to walk humbly with your God" (Mic. 6:8). Politics
can be a *spiritual* discipline and a strengthening of our commitment to the kingdom beyond our kingdoms. As many politically
experienced Christians testify, politics and religion do mix,
because God has a will to do in all the earth, in all nooks and
crannies of the human community. For them, it is not too much
to say that one cannot become either a faithful Christian or a
fulfilled human being if one is not a faithful *citizen*.[21]

We must carry on church programs to the same ends. Modern economic systems are the largest in human history. They are
getting larger. The socialist and capitalist models of economic
development apply, in the eyes of their promoters, to the whole
human world. Powerful technologies and organizational skills,
unprecedented in history, now make the idea of a "global economy" only too real. Shortages of food and energy afflict billions
of people overnight. One country like Saudi Arabia can turn off
its oil pipelines, and all Europe is in crisis. In late 1982, twenty-
six countries of the world had amassed a total debt to western
governments and banks of four hundred billion dollars. The
largest of these debtors was Mexico, whose oil resources had not
saved it from a brush with disastrous inflation which jeopard-
ized its ability to pay its international debt, sent the price of corn
wildly upwards, and swelled the tide of illegal immigration into
the United States across the Rio Grande. Should the twenty-six
countries default on their colossal debt, said Flora Lewis in the
summer of 1982, our global economy would be rocked by "a
crash that would wreck all of us."[22]

The sheer scale of economic relations in today's society
tempts us all to feelings of helplessness in the face of giant

uncontrollable forces. What can the church do in the midst of it all? Who are we to suppose we can do anything at all? Again, we are the folk who have been taught by our Lord to pray and to live in a certain way. We believe that "nothing will be able to separate us from the love of God in Christ Jesus our Lord" (Rom. 8:39), and that includes global economic systems. The freedom to search with our neighbors for new embodiments of global freedom and justice is the privilege of those who already hail God's kingdom "from afar" (Heb. 11:13).

This is basic justification of the research institutes, the conferences, and the studies of social change that characterize church programs in many parts of the world today. The new economies of scale are not beyond our understanding or our critical evaluations. But as we have frequently noted here, in economic and political affairs, Christians do not live by prayer or by study alone. Neither do we live only by plunging into secular life, saying farewell to the life of the church. The church has its own witness to society through its ministry of service to the poor.

We must neither underrate nor overrate this ministry. In the first year of his administration, President Ronald Reagan called upon "the private sector" of American society (business, churches, voluntary social service agencies) to take up the slack of federal budget cutbacks affecting poor Americans. Someone calculated that, in order for these private organizations to underwrite all these cuts in human service programs, their budgets would have to rise overnight by one hundred and forty-seven percent! No business leader or church treasurer in the tough economy of the early nineteen-eighties could do more than smile at such a proposal. The trend among some American politicians towards letting the needs of the poor fall upon non-governmental, charitable shoulders merits suspicion from Christians who believe that government, too, has a part in the "economy" of the divine kingdom. Only government can take account of the needs of all the citizens in a country, state, or county. Its obligations to serve all citizens may limit its ability to reach people with certain special needs; and here the "private sector" may always have a crucial contribution to make to real justice and real mercy for all the people of a community. But real justice and real mercy are the goals of a humane society: whether a public or a private agency does the job is not the primary point. Getting that job done is the point.

The church in history has often performed a pioneering role for government in this connection. Internationally, missionary projects and indigenous church projects have often set precedents of human service that organizations like the United Nations later incorporated into their programs of economic and social development.[23] In the history of the United States, churches sponsored emergency food programs, hospitals, orphanages, settlement houses for the immigrant poor, and job-search services decades before any government devoted tax money to such purposes. Americans live now in a country whose majority, a generation ago, conceded that government on all levels does have some responsibility for many of these human needs. We may debate the appropriate distribution of government, business, church, and other agency involvements in meeting the needs; we may ask if the federal government should spend more or less than twenty percent of our rich country's Gross National Product on these needs; and as Christians we may have to express anguished outrage at a government's refusal to cut military budgets along with budgets for the poor; but we are not likely to go back to a time when the pursuit of social justice was largely absent from the agenda of governmental tradition.

In this new situation, the responsibility of the American church is new, too. On the one hand, our ministry to the poor may have to become more concentrated on needs still neglected by the rest of society. On the other hand, we may have to broaden that ministry to link it to the formation of policy and the use of financial resources by government and business. In South India, for example, the Mar Thoma and Syrian Orthodox churches are rightly concerned for the question of land distribution among the small farmers of India. At the same time these two churches have recently undertaken together a program of building homes for some of these farmers as gifts to them. In my own current neighborhood of Upper West Side Manhattan, churches and neighborhood groups aided by federal housing monies have helped to rehabilitate an aging hotel to make it fit as apartments for aging people. More dramatically, in our neighboring borough of Brooklyn, a coalition of thirty-six local congregations from a broad spectrum of denominations has worked for four years on a "Nehemiah Plan" for rebuilding several Brooklyn neighborhoods. These neighborhoods have been as devastated by the "natural" working of urban housing economics as Jerusalem was devastated by the Babylonians before Nehemiah's reconstruction.[24] The Brooklyn Nehemiah Plan calls for the construction of five thousand townhouses for occupancy by families of low and moderate income. For the building of the first thousand of these homes, a loan fund of twelve million dollars has been put together from the thirty-six congregations and various denominations. With this "challenge fund" in hand, the church leaders went to the local New York City government with a request for an additional loan fund of ten million dollars. At City Hall, reported *The New York Times*, the request met with astonishment.

> Charles Reiss, a deputy commissioner of the Department of Housing Preservation and Development, explained the city's participation by saying: "No group has ever come to us like that before. Basically, they said, 'We've got our $12 million; what have you got?' What else could we say?"
> Deputy Mayor Robert F. Wagner, Jr., remarked: "You have a community that is willing to sacrifice and a group of churches and religious leaders who are working to rebuild a neighborhood that's been enormously devastated. It makes sense for the city to try to help."

As this is written, no one knowledgeable about the problem of affordable housing in American cities can be sure that the Nehemiah Plan in Brooklyn should be yet counted a success story. As one housing expert commented soberly:

> "They haven't got the remaining 4,000 homes covered yet. . . . They're going to need more money to build more homes, and

it's not clear now where that's going to come from. The Federal
government has disappeared as a housing-aid resource, and
Albany is a poor man's town. ..." [But, said he] "The 1000
homes are a good starting point—big enough to convince people
that the effort is not a toy but small enough to be manageable."[25]

As New York's huge housing needs go, the Brooklyn project
may still be only a token effort. But it is a token, a living anticipation, of a human community where

> My people will abide in a peaceful habitation,
> in secure dwellings, and in quiet resting places. (Isaiah 32:18)

No one who looks forward to such a community, such a kingdom, will hesitate to join forces with other citizens to make historic human cities fit for "peaceful habitation." There is a
historic human task as well as an eschatological divine promise,
when God's prophets make the prediction:

> They shall build up the ancient ruins,
> they shall raise up the former devastations;
> :hey shall repair the ruined cities,
> the devastations of many generations. (Isaiah 61:4)[26]

All who participate in the effort to rebuild even a small part
of a great city will have new prophetic agenda open up before
their eyes. City Hall, the State House, the U.S. Congress will
hear from these new Nehemiahs; for theirs must be a multi-
dimensioned ministry that carries them back and forth between
centers of social power and human need—between City Council
meetings and the sagging stairwells of corner tenements. Such
projects do not substitute for large shifts in human ways of producing wealth and distributing it in our national and global economic systems. But a church that puts all its effort into
"changing society" and none into "ministering to the poor" on
its doorsteps, is a church in danger of missing the significance
of the twice-repeated reference of the Lord's Prayer to *the day's
bread*. The short-range and the long-range of history are connected. Even episodic charity has a place in "the kingdom that
has been ready for you since the world was made" (Matt. 25:34,

NEB). In that final judgment of "the nations"[27] the leaders of business, government, and churches in America will have to answer on both counts: did you shelter people on so much as one cold night? and did you build houses for them so that they should not be cold again?

We must engage in this struggle ecumenically. An ecumenical coalition makes sense for doing, something about human problems in the great, complex cities of America. A worldwide church is none too large for ministering to similar problems of the human community as a whole. We know that the Lord's Prayer is a profoundly ecumenical prayer. It spans the world. Our ethics and our strategies of ministry must span it, too.

Struggles against *apartheid* in South Africa, political repression in Argentina, and political-religious repression in South Korea, for example, all call for the witness of the world church. The current case of South Korea is especially important for many American Christians; for on that country the church and the government of the United States have had enormous impact, for good and ill, over the past thirty-five years. South Korea, a country of some thirty-five million people, has the fastest growing Christian movement in Asia. Almost twenty percent of the population is Christian. The country also has one of the fastest growing economies in Asia, aided and shaped by large foreign investments from Japan and the United States. The current South Korean government has purchased this economic growth at the price of rigid controls of wages, the repression of the right of workers to organize independent labor unions, tolerance of large discrepancies of income in the populace as a whole, and the imprisonment of persons who protest against the government on any of these counts. Several graduates of the seminary where I currently work are jobless or in jail today in Korea because they dare to call publicly for a society free enough to give workers a voice in industry and churches a right to criticize government.

This struggle of the church in South Korea to stand up for a society both free and just has met with remarkable resonance in the churches of the world. How the South Korean government must wish that the Christian movement around the world would turn a deaf ear to the Christians and their "dissidents" in the jails of Seoul! But the Christians of other countries are not deaf to the sufferings of these brothers and sisters. We are a world body of Christ, and each of us belongs to the rest of us. "If one organ suffers, they all suffer together. If one flourishes, they all rejoice together" (1 Cor. 12:26, NEB).

In the church of the twenty-first century, this mutual suffering and rejoicing must grow, deepen, and penetrate the minds and actions of Christians throughout the earth. We are called to pray the Lord's Prayer together and to teach each other what the prayer means for our work in the whole world. Which of us has no need of help from others in discovering and performing our task in the struggle for food and freedom in our respective societies? Some years ago we had a visitor to our home from the church in Sri Lanka. He was a Roman Catholic priest and a committed socialist. He talked about the ability of the surface of earth to produce enough food to feed all the human mouths on earth. The problem, he observed, is who owns the best agricultural land and who gets to use it. "The land of the United States and the Soviet Union alone," he observed, "would be sufficient to feed the world, but the Soviets and the Americans think that the land belongs to them rather than the world." I reflected on the irony that the Soviets for some years now have been buying American-grown grain, for theirs is a country rich enough to buy it whenever they have a national food shortage.

Will there ever be a day when the whole earth will sustain the whole human community? There are some mighty barriers to the coming of such a day. Whether or not the ownership of all by all should be the ultimate Christian economic vision is a question that the religions, the ideologies, the governments, and the churches of the world should ask themselves. Not to be debated among Christians, however, is *the will of God to free and to feed all people*. How we serve that divine intention we may not yet know with unanimity. But the prayer our Lord taught us commits us to that intention, commits us together, and commits us permanently.

The next petition of the Lord's Prayer addresses the largest of the barriers lying between the vision and the coming of the kingdom of God. It is the barrier of human sin.

CHAPTER 3

Our Hope for Community

During my first trip to India, thirty years ago, I took a train from Madras to Allahabad. On the way I fell into conversation with two articulate, well-educated Hindus. As we talked about our respective religions, I mentioned the Christian belief that God is at work in the world. "How can you believe that?" one said in reply. "The world is an evil place." Then we went on to discuss the world's evils, and I remarked that one Christian approach to evil, on the human level, was the forgiveness of sins. "That's another difference between us," the other said, shaking his head. "We Hindus do not believe in the forgiveness of sins." He referred to the doctrine of *karma*.

I cannot speak with any expertness on the nature of the other great world religions; but I know that, as long as the Christian faith has been in this world, it has been a faith with one major remedy for the undoubted evil in the world: the remedy of forgiveness. The testimony of the ancient church is abundant on the point:

> God was in Christ reconciling the world to himself, not counting their trespasses against them. (2 Corinthians 5:19)

> Be kind to one another, tenderhearted, forgiving one another, as God in Christ forgave you. (Ephesians 4:32)

> [Christians] love all men, and are persecuted by all men. . . . they are reviled and they bless. They are insulted, and they do honor. When they do good, they are punished as evildoers; when they are punished, they rejoice as though they were being made alive.[1]

> Our very righteousness . . . is yet in this life of such a kind that it consists rather in the remission of sins than in the perfecting of virtues. Witness the prayer of the whole City of God in its pil-

grim state, for it cries to God by the mouth of its members, "Forgive us our debts as we forgive our debtors."[2]

Summarizing the worldview and lifestyle of early Christians, the Canadian scholar Charles N. Cochrane said:

> What is emphasized is the fact that [the Christian] has entered into a world governed not by fear or distrust but by love—a world from which the divisions and oppositions of secular society have vanished and there is neither Jew nor Greek, bond nor free. The consequence is a new sense of community which finds expression in mutual service.[3]

We have already entered into that "new sense of community" when we utter the first words of the Lord's Prayer. We enter it when we pray with all our neighbors for "our daily bread." But we enter the peculiar inner court of Christian community when we utter the forgiveness petition. To the peculiarity of that petition let us devote our attention.

The Uniqueness of the Forgiveness Petition

Greek scholars tell us that the early part of the Lord's Prayer has verbs in the aorist imperative, a tense that pitches forward into the future, suggesting the eschatological yearning of the Spirit (cf. Rom. 8:18–25). One might even translate and interpret the prayer like this:

> Thy name, Father, may it be hallowed! (By you, if not by us, for we hallow it poorly.)

> Thy kingdom, let it come! (How long it seems delayed in coming.) Thy will, let it be done on earth! (For we are far from seeing it done. Hasten the time. Shorten our wait for the perfection of your will for earth.)

> Our bread for today and tomorrow, give it to us! (For down to the very end, we are needy creatures of yours.)

Then the petition, "Forgive us our debts as we forgive our debtors." The second "forgive" in Matthew should probably be translated "have forgiven" and in Luke, "are now forgiving." Thus occurs a shift in tense, betokening a spiritual change that raises a theological problem.

The tense-shift is from verbs brimful of the future to verbs fully in the present. It is as though we had our eyes refocused suddenly from a far horizon to the place in the road where we are now standing. "Forgive us our sins, Father, as fully and as completely as we stand in a relation of forgiveness with our neighbors." The theological problem connected to this shift comes to our attention in the remarkable postlude to the prayer in Matthew 6:14–15. It is the *only* part of the prayer about which Jesus thinks it necessary to add a word of interpretation:

> "For if you forgive others the wrongs they have done, your heavenly Father will also forgive you; but if you do not forgive others, then the wrongs you have done will not be forgiven by your Father." (Matthew 6:14–15, NEB)

Many Christians down through the ages have puzzled over this word of interpretation; but none more than those who call themselves Protestant, Reformed, and Evangelical. Here Jesus seems flatly to contradict the doctrine of his disciple Paul, justification by faith. The "Paul" in many of us wants to *rewrite* the Matthew version of the Lord's Prayer at this point. Would it not be more Pauline to pray, "Forgive us our debts, Father, and then we will have the grace to forgive our debtors"? First the divine-human relationship, then the derivative human-human relationship: is that not better Christian theology? If God's dealings with us are simply a response to our dealings with each other, how different is that from the tit-for-tat law of *karma*?

Before we let our theological anxieties multiply, however, it is appropriate to put the whole issue in the context of other teachings and other events in the life of Jesus. The first sections of the Sermon on the Mount overflow with teachings about forgiveness between people who have suffered offense from each other. A grievance remembered at the start of one's formal worship in church must be resolved quickly before the worship is continued (Matt. 5:23–24). Forgiveness and the spirit of reconciliation are a better strategy for dealing with human conflict than courts of law (Matt. 5:25). The law of retaliation—"eye for an eye, tooth for a tooth"—must give way to all sorts of generosity (Matt. 5:38–42); and, most radically of all, the old human habit—"hate your enemy"—must be undone and replaced by the new rule, "Love your enemies and pray for those who persecute you so that you may be [children] of your Father who is in heaven; for he makes his sun rise on the evil and on the good, and sends rain on the just and on the unjust. . . . You, therefore, must be perfect, as your heavenly Father is perfect" (Matt. 5:43–48).

We know from other events in Jesus' ministry that forgiveness in his teaching and actions astounded and scandalized many people. Such instances as a sick man and a sinful woman (Mark 2:5; Luke 5:20, 7:48), the parable of the forgiving creditor (Luke 7:41), the unforgiving servant (Matt. 18:32), the forgiving Samaritan (Luke 10:33), the forgiving father (Luke 15:22), and the unforgiving brother (Luke 15:28) crowd the life and teaching of Jesus, impressing his contemporaries with the *central* place of forgiveness in his mission. Forgiveness was so characteristic of that mission that we can readily understand how the early church came to believe that among Jesus' final words from the cross were, "Father, forgive them . . ." (Luke 23:34). Those words cannot be found in the earliest New Testament manuscripts, but forgiveness can be found as a centerpiece of Christian theology and ethics from early times indeed. As one commentator says, "The scribe who inserted it did so with a deep and true understanding of the Galilean teacher. It is one of the most typically 'Christian' utterances credited to Jesus in the gospel tradition."[4]

The pervasiveness of this theme in the Gospel narratives gives us a clue to the alleged conflict between Pauline theology and the Lord's Prayer. The teachings of Jesus and the theology of Paul both conform to the summary principle of Christian ethics in the writings of John: "We love, because he first loved us" (1 John 4:19). The generous love of the Creator lies all around you in the flowers, the grass, the birds, says Jesus early in the Sermon on the Mount. God lavishes the gifts of creation—rain, sun, food—upon the whole of humanity. You are *surrounded* from the beginning of your life by the uncalculating love of the Creator of the world. Just so, the divine mercy infuses human relations most at those moments when debts are cancelled, hurts are healed, and just resentments are forgotten. There is a new life to be lived here, an entry into a "world governed not by fear or distrust but by love" (in Cochrane's phrase). There is a *reality* to be touched and enjoyed, a new set of relations between God and his children, a seamless robe of relations at once Godly and human. It is as though Jesus were saying to his disciples, "You cannot know or enjoy the mercy of God in one dimension without knowing it in others. If you are going to live by the generosity of God your Father, you will have to live generously alongside your fellow creatures. You may try to live by the law of retaliation in an eye-for-eye legalistic mode of relation to your neighbors. But if you do, you will sever yourself from the world of divine kindness. To step inside the circle of that kindness is to come accompanied by your neighbors! Try leaving *them*, and you leave *me*." The most eloquent picture of this viewpoint is Jesus' parable of the forgiving father and his two sons in Luke 15. We read that the elder brother "was angry and refused to go in" to the party celebrating the prodigal's return. We do not know if he ever went in. If he did not, he was outside the father's house forever. The viewpoint of Jesus and the whole New Testament is that only one who loves brother and sister "abides in the light" while one who hates brother or sister already "walks in the darkness" (1 John 2:10–11).

"Love" is a large word for the relation of God and God's creatures on the lips of Jesus, the apostles, and the early Christians. To avoid the sentimentality and subjectivism often associated with that word in its *English* usage, we do well to remember that the heart of love, in Jesus and all the apostles, is *forgiveness*. The disciple prays to God while already living in the relation of forgiveness towards neighbors all around. The life of the kingdom of God rests on a ground nourished by the air and the rain of forgiveness, the most distinct and indispensable of all the gifts of the Holy Spirit![5]

The New Testament is clear about this basic ingredient of forgiveness in the Christian faith and ethic. Less clear is the meaning of forgiveness in modern society, especially in the face of certain criticisms directed against the ethic of forgiveness by skeptics ancient and modern. I have discovered, as a pastor and as a teacher, that modern Christians misunderstand forgiveness along with many of their contemporaries. In order to study closely what it really means to pray, "forgive us our debts," we may have to understand those who do *not* want to pray that way. If we understand their reasons for resisting the very notion of forgiveness, we might understand better a similar resistance, deep down in ourselves. More: we might discover deeper down, the joy of those who do learn, in spirit and in truth, to pray this petition.

Three Objections to the Forgiveness of Sins

In the history of Christian debate with other religious and ethical points of view, three major criticisms of forgiveness ethics have surfaced. One group of critics claims that forgiveness is ethically *wrong*; another, that it is pragmatically *useless*; and a third that it is personally *degrading*. Let us reflect on these three in turn.

Is forgiveness wrong, because it offends against justice? From the Pharisees scandalized at Jesus' lenient treatment of "a woman who was leading an immoral life" (Luke 7:37, NEB) to the writing of the philosopher Immanuel Kant in eighteenth-century Europe, the forgiveness of sins has been under attack from some very thoughtful and morally serious people. The gist of their criticism is that forgiveness offends against justice, because it treats wrongdoing with less-than-ultimate seriousness.

Ordinary citizens join the ranks of these critics everytime they cry out for "justice" in the treatment of proven criminals. By justice they mean some form of the law of retribution. We had a painful discussion of retribution versus forgiveness not long ago in my neighborhood in New York City. We were confronted anew with something of the scandal, shock, and near intolerability of forgiveness in human affairs. Hugh McEvoy, a young man of sixteen, a member of a parish church just across the street from

Union Seminary, was murdered by another young man, barely thirteen years old, in a senseless unprovoked act of violence. On the very day of the funeral, the father of the murdered boy, Mr. Leo McEvoy, said to a reporter of *The New York Times*:

> "My faith in religion is one of forgiveness, turn the other cheek. . . . It's what one has to do as a Christian, but it's not easy to do."

McEvoy, a practicing Roman Catholic, knows one of the implications of his belief about forgiveness for public policy in the treatment of criminals. He went on to say:

> "My own personal belief goes along with [New York] Governor Carey's. I don't believe in capital punishment. I do believe in life imprisonment."[6]

McEvoy is a professional probation officer. He works everyday with people convicted of crimes who have been given a chance to "go straight" again. Punishment for wrongdoing he still believes in. We are not, in his view, permitted by our faith to adopt a superficial attitude that says, "Think nothing of it!" (Actually, as we shall see, forgiveness involves thinking, feeling, doing very *much* about "it"—the wrong of which humans are capable.) Some sharp edges of doubt remain, however, especially as one views with horror a crime like this one. How well we understand cries for revenge against murderers and all enemies of public safety:

> "If we don't punish crime, how can we truly oppose it?"

> "If criminals know that they will be forgiven, how do we protect their potential future victims?"

> "What *right* do we have to overlook a crime against a neighbor or against ourselves? Is it not our first and continuing obligation *not* to overlook it? *Not* to 'let it go'?"

The usual word for "forgive" in the New Testament means "let go." As the word "debts" in the Matthew version of the Lord's Prayer reminds us, to "let go" a debt is to give up something that is *owed* to you. The critics of forgiveness object *morally* to any backing-off from "collection of debts." "What kind of a world would it be," they protest, "if you could borrow money without being obliged to pay it back? Or harm a neighbor without being obliged to effect restoration? Or commit any wrong act and not have your guilt affirmed and punished? You may be a good-hearted person, Mr. McEvoy, but you are soft-hearted and soft-headed! If it is 'Christian' to forgive, then maybe Christians are *wrong*."

How shall we reply to this line of argument?

First, here are some features of the ethics of the Old and New Testaments that are *not* violated or cancelled by the forgiveness of sins:

> —the *horror* and revulsion of God against some evils that humans commit in the world. (Nobody "hates sin" as deeply and as steadily as does the God and Father of Jesus Christ.)

> —the *judgment* of God against the evils of human behavior. (Jesus made it clear that all sorts of human sin—adultery, murder, thievery, extortion, greed, oppression of the poor, religious hypocrisy and spiritual pride—fall under the judgment of God.)

> —the *repentance and restitution* that must be assumed as a true response to the forgiveness of a sin whose results, in the lives of the sinner and the sinned-against, must be taken as seriously as the offense itself.

A thorough study of forgiveness in both testaments will show, in fact, that all these elements—horror at wrong, judgment against it, and the demand for restitution—are involved or implied in any act of forgiveness, divine or human. One cannot, for example, "forgive" a sin that has not already been identified *as* a sin. Far from being merely an act of "letting go," an act of forgetting, forgiveness is first an act of profound *remembering*. If Jesus said from the cross, "Father forgive them, for they know not what they do," we may be sure that *he* knew what they were doing, and *God* knew, too! To the sum total of human guilt for that crucifixion was thus added guilt for gross ignorance. (As we shall see in the third group of critics below, the judgmental element in forgiveness offends them, while this first group, good moralists that they are, insists on the necessity of judgment against sin.)

The clash of opinion between Christians and moralists here does not, in fact, focus on the question of moral judgment. The question is: between God and humans, between humans themselves, is there any action towards wrong *beyond* judgment? The overwhelming answer of the New Testament is "yes." The difference between the two viewpoints really comes to rest in differing views of God's nature, God's relation to humans, fundamental social righteousness, and the good of human society. The real quarrel is theological.[7] In the Lord's Prayer we pray that God's "will be done on earth as it is in heaven." What is that will? That human wrongdoing be identified, resisted, punished? So far, yes. But not far enough:

God wills the restoration of broken creature relations—divine-human and human-human. God is not only a moral judge of the world; God is even more the moral restorer of the world. The basic criticism to be made of the moral critics is that they value judgment against sin more than the healing of sinners and relations broken by sin.

In the language of western philosophy and theology, the rejection of the notion of forgiveness by a thinker like Kant arises from a rational, abstract ethic rather than a concrete, redemptive ethic. Are we to worship a God who knows only how to maintain anger against evil, or one who also knows how to heal the relationships whose brokenness provokes the anger? There is no doubt about Jesus' stand on this question. There should be no doubt in the minds and hearts of those who pray as he taught us to pray. The world has a Creator who governs it by a law more powerful than the laws of karma, revenge, and thermodynamics. God loves the world enough to heal it. *That* is the theological point on which forgiveness rests, and on that point Christians can brook no intellectual or spiritual compromise.

Is forgiveness useless, because it focuses on the past rather than the future? The second group of critics agrees with the fundamental theological point that restitution, repentance, and healing are practical needs deserving much effort in human affairs.

These critics are moral pragmatists rather than moral legalists. They take evil seriously, but they take its *results* more seriously. Representative of them is the American psychologist O. Hobart Mowrer, who has called forgiveness "a profound irrelevancy in human affairs."[8] It is irrelevant, in his view, because it concerns something over and done with. A critic of this second sort might reason in this way: "Forgiveness will not bring back Leo McEvoy's son, will it? It won't benefit the martyrs of the Nazi concentration camp, will it? Or millions of black Africans killed on the Atlantic as they were transported toward America as slaves to the New World? Forgiveness is *impractical*. It seems to presuppose that something can be done to undo the grim tragedy of life, the mistakes of the past that continue to impose suffering on the present. Let us concentrate on alleviating the suffering. Let us not repeat the mistakes. Let us clear the debris of the past as well as we can, remembering that the past is dead and gone. The future alone we can do something about."

Pragmatic Americans like myself find this objection rather appealing. But experience can teach even Americans the superficiality of such a criticism. One of the places in the world where I learned to reflect on this superficiality was the city of Hiroshima in Japan. All Americans might well pay a visit to Hiroshima. We need to understand what it means to us to be the only nation so far in history to have dropped an atomic bomb on another nation. The city of Hiroshima has gathered together the discoverable names of all the victims of that bomb; and so far over one hundred thousand names have been collected in the marble container in the city's "Peace Park." Over one end of that marble is written, in Japanese, the words, "The Mistake Will Not Be Repeated." One of the intriguing things about that inscription is its ambiguity. *Whose* mistake will not be repeated? Americans of my generation are especially interested in that question. I was seventeen years old at the end of World War II. I was actually drafted into tho U.S. army six months after the dropping of the Hiroshima bomb. I could have become a part of the American army that was scheduled to invade Japan. I could even owe my life to the bombs that killed over one hundred thousand citizens of Hiroshima and almost as many citizens of Nagasaki. Such thoughts stirred me deeply in my visit to the Hiroshima Peace Park and to its museum. There, some of the horrors of atomic bombing confront the visitor in pictures, relics of explosion and fire, and statistics of damage. Throughout this museum the suffering of the Japanese people is the center of attention. Undoubtedly the museum reflects the deep resentment and suspicion of many other Asians over American readiness to drop such a bomb on an Asian country, when it did not do so on a European country. One gets the feeling from such a visit to Hiroshima that the "mistake," not to be repeated, was at least as much an American mistake as a Japanese mistake. One comes away from Hiroshima, as an American, acknowledging the continuation of guilt, resentment, hostility on *both* sides of this forty-year-old war.

The Japanese are also a very pragmatic people, and the commitment of many of them not to repeat "the mistake" must be honored and applauded by all their neighbors. But a haunting visit to Hiroshima will convince even the most pragmatic American and Japanese that James McBride Dabbs was only too right when he said, "We carry the past into the future, and it carries us."[9] The German founder of psychoanalysis, Sigmund Freud, documented this principle in the development of human personality. All of us are museums of our own past, he said. We carry in ourselves the joys and sorrows of our own childhood. Sometime our unhappiness in adulthood can be explained by our continuing "hang up" with some childhood experience. Freud compared our hang ups with a line of soldiers marching down a road. Each of us is equipped from babyhood with a certain number of soldiers. When we have a nagging problem—some hostility or anxiety that we never resolve—we "station some troops" alongside that problem. We tie up our energies there, and we lose the use of those energies for times further down the road. That is why some people, so pinned down and pulled into their own pasts, have no resources left for coping with the present. The mental hospitals of every country are filled with such persons.

If this is true of individual personalities, it is also true of the history of group conflict. The American Civil War of the 1860s is over a hundred years in our past. Not a single veteran of that war is now living in the United States. Yet, remembered resentments between southerners and northerners still smoulder in this country. It is only a smoulder, and gradually it is becoming a joke to call a fellow American a "rebel" or a "Yankee." But a short generation ago it was no joke. And for a few Americans it still is not altogether a joke. If someone killed your grandfather, the descendants of the killer are hard to forgive. What country in the world has no version of such a story to tell? How long will it take for Jews to "let go" their great justified hostility against Germans of the last generation? How long will it take before Hindus and Moslems can live together in India and across the India-Pakistan borders in something more binding than militarized "peace"? Will Arabs and Jews ever get over their memories of their wars against each other? When will the "Christian" leaders of Northern Ireland, Southern Ireland, and England acknowledge to their respective peoples that it is high time, after eight hundred years of "The Irish Question," to deliver their political relations from the vicious scourge of *vengefulness*? And when will Americans northern and southern finally concede to each other: "There were right and wrong on both sides of that 'War Between the States.' Wars are always between sinners."

Forgiveness, useless? Half the hostilities that wreck human community can be overcome only by acts of reconciliation resembling forgiveness. Forgiveness may be the most useful human action in the world! What could be more useful than a reconciliation that permits the warring segments of the human race to devote their energies to the arts of peace and prosperity?

Again we confront, in a criticism of Christian forgiveness, a difference between the Christian view of the world and other views. God means to beat swords into plowshares, to establish justice and peace in the earth; and one of God's principal ways of doing just this is the promulgation of the forgiveness of sins.

If anyone, in the Christian view, has a right to hold the world's sins against it forever, that one is God! Who could blame the just Holy God for never doing anything else but holding the world up to judgment? In fact the Holy One holds up to the world the promise of reconciliation. We who pray to this Promiser must live by that same promise.

Robert Frost has a famous poem, "Mending Wall," that puts the philosophical conflict here unforgettably. The poet meets his neighbor, a fellow farmer, at the edge of their two farms, on a day in early spring. The winter snows and ice of New England have cracked and toppled parts of the stone wall that divides the two properties. Why are you so carefully repairing the wall between us? the poet asks. The other farmer replies with a proverb, "Good fences make good neighbors." No, reflects the poet, the opposite is true.

> Before I built a wall, I'd ask to know
> What I was walling in or walling out,
> And to whom I was like to give offence.

Looking at the ice-cracked, snow-toppled stones of the winter just past, he reflects:

> Something there is that doesn't love a wall,
> That wants it down.[10]

For Christian faith that "something" is the Lord of human history, the God and Father of Jesus who in the Spirit works throughout the creation to "set it free from its bondage to decay" until it participates in "the glorious liberty of the children of God" (Rom. 8:21). What could be more practical than a power that will overcome the justified hostilities that humans bear against each other from the past, liberating them to community with each other? Forgiveness is that liberation.

Is forgiveness degrading, because it subjects another to judgment and kindness? This final criticism is the most superficial of the three. It operates from a pole opposite the first criticism, which was chiefly concerned to keep moral principle firm. The third critic's counterclaim may go like this: "Forgiveness is an act whereby one person or group visits indignity upon another. It reminds other people that they are sinners, puts them in a position of inferiority to the forgiver, and subjects them to generosity. It is demeaning, patronizing, and imperialistic. What do you mean, you 'forgive' my sins? Suppose I don't want to be forgiven? Suppose I don't even agree that I have any sins to be forgiven?"

I can imagine a version of this objection coming from some of my neighbors in Hiroshima. If I should speak, as an American, about our country's "forgiveness" of Japan's sins against us I can imagine the Japanese replying, "Ah so? who has more forgiving to do? What wrongs did we ever do America that you should discriminate against us in your trade and immigration policies before the war? And if we did wrongs to you, did we deserve the atomic bomb? If you want to talk about forgiveness, you had better get some agreement on what there is on *both* sides to forgive!"

In the human social situation, where the sinners belong to both sides and forgiveness therefore must flow in both directions, my hypothetical Japanese friend is quite correct: we need some agreements on both sides about (a) the sins to be forgiven, and (b) the readiness of each side to forgive and/or be forgiven. The complex dynamic of an act of forgiveness requires all this. On biblical grounds we know that an act of forgiveness begins in judgment, is intent on reconciliation, involves some relenting of punishment, but drives towards repentant restoration, and "newness of life." All of this *does* imply a certain imbalance of relations between sinner and sinned-against, and the third critic is right to perceive that a certain kind of indignity is involved. Another name for *resistance* to this indignity is *pride*, one of the classic seven deadly sins of Christian tradition. Critics of this third group walk on the thin edge of moral pride when they bristle at the idea of their being under judgment for their misdeeds. On this point John Wesley had the correct *ad hominem* argument in a conversation with General Oglethorpe, governor of the new American colony of Georgia. "I never forgive," exclaimed Oglethorpe. "Then I hope, sir," replied Wesley, "you never sin."[11]

Is the New Testament correct or in error when it claims, "All have sinned and fall short of the glory of God" (Rom. 3:23)? Are we all in fact the subjects as well as the objects of wrong action? Do we in fact suffer both alienations of sinning and being sinned against? If the answer to these questions is an easy-going, "Not necessarily," then the forgiveness of sins might well be dismissed as *both* useless and undignified. If on the other hand evil-doing and evil-suffered are common to us all, we have already undergone the collapse of our true dignity as human beings. A murderer and a liar, a hypocrite and an extortioner may claim a sort of dignity; but it is the false dignity of "high-handed sin" and "pride that goeth before a fall." The *true* dignity of human being, in the Christian view, is a restoration of community, the happiest possible aftermath of a relation broken by wrong. In one's experience of such a restoration, one can become content with subjection to the kindness of God and a neighbor. In that experience, one can know what Augustine meant when he said: "There is something in humility that lifts up the head."

Such humility is all the more appropriate in that double-relation of forgiving required by the Lord in his prayer: "Forgive us . . . as we have forgiven." Who, living in a relation of forgiveness from the all-righteous, all-merciful God, will practice forgiveness towards a neighbor in a demeaning, imperialistic fashion? On the human level, especially in the church, we are commanded to "be kind to one another, tenderhearted, forgiving one another as God in Christ forgave [us]" (Eph. 4:32), for all of us have reasons to be forgiven and all of us pray to the Father to forgive us. Critics of the third group are not well acquainted with the Christian experience. Sin in us all is more real, the love of God is more dignifying and liberating, and the humility of the forgiven is more joyful than they suppose.

Postscript and Prelude: The Restored Human Community

Some years ago I scratched my new desk, a handsome

piece of furniture made of fine teakwood. My secretary heard my expressions of dismay and she called out cheerily, "Oh, don't worry about it. My husband and I have a boat with a deck made of teak. You will find that it is a very forgiving wood. You just rub it with steel wool and put teak oil over it, and you will hardly see the scratch." The label on my bottle of teak oil more or less confirmed her opinion: "Genuine teakwood becomes more beautiful the older it gets and the more it is used. But please treat it kindly: do not soak it in water, or place it in the dishwasher. Rub it clean with a damp cloth from time to time."

Forgiveness may not come as easily to human relations as it does to teakwood, but in both cases it is good to know that many, if not all, breaks in their integrity are repairable. If they were not, how could any human community have lasted this long? Only shallow thinkers will accuse the New Testament writers of underestimating the damage that humans are capable of inflicting on each other or the cost of repairing that damage. Damaged as it is, our world is a grim place already. It would be yet grimmer if repairs were never possible.

The promise of repair does not make us careless about doing the good we have power to do. Better *not* to "soak it in water," better to have fewer repairs to make. But flaws in human relations are tragic perennial facts. Whether, after cruel rupture, some human communities can be put back together again is a practical political question in all ages of history. For politics has to do with the fractures and the re-forming of our relations to each other as a public.

As it prays the Lord's Prayer, the church, by God's intention, is to be a parable of the restored human community. "Behold how they love one another" was testimony of outsiders to the "new thing" evident in the very early Christian church. Forgiveness between sinners is so unusual that it seems new whenever it happens. Most human associations depend upon people's liking for each other. The association promised by the gospel will be for people who may not like each other but who claim association anyway. Such a community will resemble "relatives" as Kurt

Vonnegut describes them from his own family: "Relatives aren't there to be liked. They're there to be relatives."[12]

The church is a company of forgiven forgivers. One becomes a member of the church by joining others in the corporate confession, "While we were yet sinners Christ died for us" (Rom. 5:8). As a community based in the forgiveness of sins, the church, by the grace of God, can be a parable of the "healing of nations"—nations mired down in war, preparation for war, and every form of collective hostility known to human politics. Revenge shouts very loudly in much human political life. Forgiveness seems to wait quietly outside the courts of power for a reconciliation that is never the order of the day. It waits, too, outside the walls of church bodies who have yet to forgive each other for the sins of their respective ecclesiastical ancestors. The struggle of Christians to pray their Lord's Prayer faithfully could well begin in a new commitment to visible church unity in the body of Christ. "Behold how they scorn one another!" is the justified response of many outsiders to the unending divisions of churches around the world.

In any of its gatherings and especially around its communion table, the church celebrates a reconciliation that has already come to this world, that no faithlessness in the church or in human politics can destroy. "God was in Christ reconciling the world to himself, not counting their trespasses against them, and entrusting to us the message of reconciliation" (2 Cor. 5:19)—to us, the sinful church! But unless the forgiveness of sins prevails at least in our churchly affairs we shall have betrayed that amazing divine trust in us. We shall have no distinctive Christian witness to render in secular politics, for nothing is more distinctive about Christian social ethics than the forgiveness of sins. Having faulted in that trust—having yielded to the unforgiving spirit inside the church—we take ourselves outside the realm of reconciliation. We make ourselves strangers to the kingdom of God.

As surely as a refusal to feed our hungry neighbors with bread, a refusal to live forgivingly with our sinful neighbors will make it impossible for us to hear the word of the last judgment:

"You have my Father's blessing . . ." (Matt. 25:34, NEB). For we will have stepped outside the realm of blessedness where human sinners pray together: "Forgive us our debts, as we also have forgiven our debtors."

CHAPTER 4

On the Way to the Coming Kingdom

We began this study of the Lord's Prayer with two questions: who first prayed this prayer? and to whom did they pray it? Let us begin to end it by asking: *when* did they pray it?

Though Jesus taught the disciples to "pray like this" during his ministry with them, they almost certainly did not pray the prayer as a group until after the crucifixion and resurrection. They took these words on their lips only

> —after they had heard other prayer from Jesus' lips in his ministry, in Gethsemane, on the cross;
>
> —after he had broken bread with them on the road to Emmaus and prayed with them in his post-crucifixion presence;
>
> —after they had shared in the power of the resurrection, the Holy Spirit, and joined each other in *koinonia* in the Spirit, the church.[1]

In short, they began to pray the Lord's Prayer not just as the remembered teaching of one long dead but as the words of one triumphantly alive, with the Father, in the Spirit, with the church, in the world.

Just as the prayer took on new meaning in light of the completed ministry of Jesus, it also took on new meaning in light of the ongoing ministry and mission of the early church. We have seen how they went before the Roman courts, went to jail, went even to execution, all because they insisted on doing just what the first petition of the Prayer asked to be done: "Hallowed be thy name." They went to prison and to death because they refused to equate the will of humans with the will of God. "Thy will be done" meant defiance, on occasion, of human wills. An early example of this is the prayer of Simon Peter after being hauled into a Jerusalem court:

> "And now, Lord, look upon their threats, and grant to thy servants to speak thy word with all boldness, while thou stretchest out thy hand to heal, and signs and wonders are performed through the name of thy holy servant Jesus." (Acts 4:29)

They also learned early to bless God for "daily bread" in their first common worship and common meals as a church (cf. Acts 2:42); and there never was a more literal conformity to the forgiveness petition than the one recorded of Stephen in his dying breath: "Lord, do not hold this sin against them" (Acts 7:60).

Even so, over centuries of effort to be faithful disciples, the church uttered the final petition:

> "Lead us not into temptation,
> But deliver us from evil."

Before asking what that petition may mean, let us note that the Lord's Prayer originally *ended* right there. There is hardly any doubt, from manuscript study, that the words, "For thine is the kingdom, the power, and the glory, forever" entered the prayer in church liturgy beginning in the late first century and continuing on a wide scale through subsequent centuries. These were the centuries of persecution, missionary expansion, and the church's passage from being a minority sect to being the official religion of the declining Roman empire. Since the doxology appears in the late first-century writing, *Didache*, we can say that soon after the Apostolic era the church had added these words to the briefer prayer as uttered by Jesus.[2] The doxology clearly did not originate with Jesus. It originated in the church.

In fidelity to modern Scripture-study, therefore, should modern Christians omit the doxology from our utterance of the prayer? Only a certain biblical literalism would say so. The ending of prayer with praise had solid Jewish precedent. It returns the mind of the worshiper to the same focus on the greatness of God with which prayer rightly begins. Furthermore, precisely since the echo of the faithful church sounds in these words, who are we, heirs of that faithfulness, to silence it? This is the prayer that Christians sang on their way to jail and stammered with their dying breaths before their execution. Like the *Kaddish* sung by many a Jew on the way to the medieval Inquisition or Nazi death camp, this prayer has stood the utmost tests of human devotion. Only sheer ingratitude and historical ignorance would impel anyone to ban these words from the contemporary liturgies of the church.[3]

In the Greek text of the Lord's Prayer, a shift occurs in the doxology that, spiritually speaking, resembles the shift from climbing a mountain to standing at last upon its summit. As we have seen, almost all the verbs of the prayer (most notably in Matthew's version) are Greek aorist imperatives. There is strain, struggle, yearning in these aorist tenses. The verbs overflow with eschatological hope, with the inspired impatience of those who have not yet "received what was promised" but have seen it and "greeted it from afar" as a reality sure someday to come (Heb. 11:13).

> For we know that all the creation has been groaning and travailing up to the present moment; and not only the creation, but we ourselves, who have the firstfruits of the Spirit, are also groaning inwardly as we await our adoption as God's children, the liberation of our body. For we have been saved in hope. ... (Romans 8:23–24a, author's translation)

In sum, the entire prayer, down to the doxology, leans towards a liberated human future, towards that time when

> The divine name will be truly hallowed,
> the divine kingdom truly come,
> the divine will perfectly done;

a time when we shall see

> the human need for sustenance fulfilled at the great, joyful
>   heavenly Banquet,
> our last sin forgiven,
> our last temptation resisted,
> and evil defeated once and for all.

Then, *then* all the saints and all the powers of creation will join the chorus of the kingdom come and indicative moods and declarative sentences can take over human language for ever and ever:

> The sovereignty of the world has passed to our Lord and his Christ, and he shall reign for ever and ever! (Revelation 11:15, NEB)

> For thine is the kingdom and the power and the glory, forever. Amen!

That time is not yet. If we add the doxology to the Lord's Prayer, along with the early church, we are leaping ahead, so to speak, to claim our places in the hallelujah chorus of the end-time. *All* times and tenses have their home in this prayer: the past (we have forgiven our debtors), the present (we need bread daily) and the future (the coming kingdom) belong to us, because in Jesus and in the Spirit that raised him from the dead, we belong to God.

In the Meantime?

In the meantime, temptation and evil are the crises of discipleship. In most of what follows I want to think about the crises of modern discipleship in relation to the last petition, but first let's wrestle with an obvious theological problem: what does it mean to ask God not to *lead* us into temptation?

Karl Barth called this a "fearful prayer," and no phrase in it strikes most of us with more fear than this. Ought we to fear that God will lead us right into the very jaws of temptation?[4] Is God the sort of Power who "tests" our ability to withstand opportunities for infidelity? If so, there may be something evil in God to fear. But surely that is not Jesus' meaning. A proper context of interpretation is the life of Jesus himself and the perceptions of the disciples about that life. Especially in their memories of what Jesus endured on the way to his own death, the disciples had vivid images of real temptation. At some point in his teachings he recounted to them the temptations that beset him at the very beginning of his public ministry as he was "led by the Spirit for forty days in the wilderness, tempted by the devil" (Luke 4:1–2; cf. Matt. 4:1–11; Mark 1:12–13). Here an

evil power does the "tempting" but a Holy Spirit does the "lend-
ing." Remarkably, the subjects of these crucial early temptations
relate intimately to the sweep of the Lord's Prayer—bread,
political power, the true worship of God, and the presumption
of facing *God* with a human-generated temptation. Temptation
assaulted Jesus throughout his ministry but especially in connection with his death. A loyal disciple, Simon Peter, recognizes
the peculiar authority of Jesus as God's Chosen One (Matt.
16:17), and then recoils in horror at the thought that Jesus will
soon "be killed." But such recoiling is more work of the
demonic tempter, replies Jesus to the thunderstruck disciple:
"Get behind me, Satan!" (Matt. 16:23). Again, the disciples
remember that Jesus tried unsuccessfully to persuade them to
participate in prayer with him as he faces the very death he
knew was coming:

> "Watch and pray that you may not enter into temptation; the
> spirit indeed is willing, but the flesh is weak." Again, for the sec-
> ond time, he went away and prayed. "My Father, if this cannot
> pass unless I drink it, thy will be done." And again he came and
> found them sleeping, for their eyes were heavy. So, leaving
> them again, he went away and prayed for the third time, saying
> the same words. (Matthew 26:41–49)

> And there appeared to him an angel from heaven, strengthen-
> ing him. And being in an agony he prayed more earnestly; and
> his sweat became like great drops of blood falling down upon
> the ground. And when he rose from prayer, he came to the dis-
> ciples and found them sleeping for sorrow, and he said to them,
> "Why do you sleep? Rise and pray that you may not enter into
> temptation." (Luke 22:43–46)

And two of the Gospel writers record that in the final moments
of Jesus' death-agony, on the terrible margin between faith in
God and faithlessness, he cried out with the Psalmist: "My God
my God, why hast thou forsaken me?" (Matt. 27:46; Mark
15:34; cf. Ps. 22:1ff.).

During their three years of "basic training" with him, therefore, the disciples had some clear lessons in the difference
between *his* and *their* capacity to endure and resist temptation.

When he so taught them to pray, did Jesus already have in mind the limits of the disciples' ability to withstand the very temptations he himself was getting ready to endure? In the case of Simon Peter, we know that he had precisely this in mind. Forever after, the church, remembering the difference between Jesus and Peter, *identified* with Peter. "Father, test us not as Jesus was tested, for we, like Peter, are weak. But deliver us from evil as Jesus and Peter were both delivered!"

The great spiritual point of the petition is our rightful fear and trembling about our strength as disciples. Hope and trust in God alone can really see us through temptations and evils beyond our power to resist. If the forgiveness petition squarely identifies what lies within the power of the disciples—to forgive each other's sins—the final petition squarely identifies what does *not* lie within that power. Indeed scholarly uncertainty about the translation of "evil" in the text reminds us of this very fact. Should the words *tou ponerou* be translated "the evil" or "the evil one"—i.e., the Satanic power? No certain answer can be given, but we can be sure that Jesus had such respect for the evil in the world that he trusted *God* to overcome that evil, as the great cry of trust from the cross witnesses:

"Father, into your hands I commit my spirit." (Luke 23:46)

The sequel to that cry was resurrection!

The summary point is that there is evil in the world that we have the power to overcome—such as the evil of an unforgiving spirit. Then there is evil in the world that we have limited power to resist, and concerning that power we can only pray that God will be our present strength in time of trouble. We do well to remind ourselves and the world at the end, therefore, that the "power and the glory" really do belong to our great Deliverer.

Into What Temptations Must We Pray Not to Be Led?

The time was October 1962. The United States and the U.S.S.R. were locked in conflict over the Soviet intention to install ballistic missiles in Cuba, ninety miles from Florida. It was the world's most serious approach to nuclear confrontation, and large numbers of people in Washington, Moscow, and other world capitals were deeply fearful. During the week of this international crisis, people in the United States attended churches in larger numbers than usual. The chapel at Union Theological Seminary in New York, I am told, was filled to overflowing with students, faculty, and staff members. "We didn't know what to do about the great crisis," one person reported, "but we knew we had to pray."

One of the U.S. officials in the midst of that crisis was Secretary of State Dean Rusk, who happened to be a member of the Presbyterian Church, U.S. Afterwards, someone asked him what he learned from the Cuba crisis. He replied, "I learned something about the old question of the Westminster Confession of Faith, 'What is the chief end of man?' The answer is, 'To glorify God and to enjoy him forever.' " At stake in the Cuban standoff between the U.S.A. and the U.S.S.R., he seemed to say, was national safety, pride, power, and glory. National glory, Rusk suggested, can be a human highroad to disaster.

In a century when access to constructive and destructive powers has grown geometrically among humankind, we have abundant reason as Christians to pray this final petition in full awareness of its dreadful pertinence to our contemporary history. Who is not shaken to remember how the great scientific and technological advances of nineteenth-century Europe bore evil political fruit in World War I, with its killing of thirty-six million human beings to determine—among other such purposes—which European nations would have the largest colonial empires? Who needs a better image of futility than the Battle of Verdun, with its million casualties and its stalemate outcome? The twentieth century was to supply a grisly array of more such images. The "civilized" world went on to a World War II, inflicting at least as many deaths by technical refinements as diverse as airplanes, radar, gas ovens, and atomic fission. In the "peace" of the years 1945–1982, about twenty-five million more human beings have perished in war; and we stand, in year thirty-eight of the Nuclear Era, with a technology in place for making the planet earth virtually uninhabitable by humankind.

We go to movies like *Star Wars* in which we accept as entirely possible in some future world the instantaneous obliteration of a planet by an enemy's super-explosive. But we can *conceive* of that obliteration now because we know that there now rests, in missile silos in at least two countries of earth, enough super-explosives to do much the same to our own planet—on any day, like the day when you may be reading this page.

The nuclear peril is not the first or the only "temptation" and "evil" which lend historical concrete urgencies to Christians in their prayers; but it is hard to imagine a spiritually alert offering of the prayer today which ignores the perils of the so-called Atomic Era. The most eloquent recent interpreter of these perils has been Jonathan Schell, whose book, *The Fate of the Earth*, is appropriate parallel reading for any modern reflection on this last petition of our Lord's Prayer. Schell verges on theology when he writes:

> Scientific progress may yet deliver us from many evils, but there are at least two evils it cannot deliver us from: its own findings and our own destructive and self-destructive bent. This is a combination that we will have to learn to deal with by some other means.[5]

> We have no choice but to address the issue of nuclear weapons as though we knew for a certainty that their use would put an end to our species. In weighing the fate of the earth and, with it, our own fate, we stand before a mystery, and in tampering with the earth we tamper with a mystery. We are in deep ignorance. Our ignorance should dispose us to wonder, our wonder should make us humble, our humility should inspire us to reverence and caution, and our reverance and caution should lead us to act without delay to withdraw the threat we now pose to the earth and to ourselves.[6]

The connections of theology, ethics, and politics commended in this study of our Lord's Prayer match closely Schell's perspective on this moment of human history. What we know scientifically must now be combined with what we do not know politically: how to control our collective capacity for evil. Now as seldom before our human achievements must find their home again in a creation not our achievement. Out of a new "reverence and caution" in us must grow, not despair or inaction, but wiser world politics and the hopeful action of those who work for what they pray for.

The power and the glory belong to God. When we put too much confidence in our ability to control our own history, to do good, and to resist evil, we overextend ourselves. Christians must pray the final petitions of the Lord's Prayer on behalf of all humankind: lead us not into the temptation to trust ourselves; give us trust in you, O God, to deliver us from evil!

For us Christians, accurate perception of temptation comes from an amalgam of clear faith and clear sight—a correct reading of both the Bible and the newspaper. Correctly focused, this binocular vision will alert us to the age-old nature of human temptation. Not everything about modern technology and politics is unique to the twentieth century. To think so is tempting! It is still true, as it was for the Corinthian Christians to whom Paul wrote:

> No temptation has overtaken you that is not common to humans. God is faithful, and he will not let you be tempted beyond your strength, but with the temptation will also provide the way of escape, that you may be able to endure it. (1 Corinthians 10:13)

What are some of our particular temptations? Let us divide them between those that confront us spiritually in the church and those that confront us politically in the church's relation to public affairs.

Three Temptations of the Spirit

1. To stop praying. At times in human affairs the only thing we know to do is pray. Prayer is our only real resource in the face of death. Prayer alone gives us the nerve even to "think about the unthinkable"—the evils of our time that exceed our imagination with their colossal quantity and their intimidating quality: world war, death camps, global hunger, nuclear annihilation. Jesus told his disciples to *pray* for bread, forgiveness, and power to withstand temptation. Paul advised the young church at Thessalonica, "Pray constantly" (1 Thess. 5:17). Here, official Marxism has an unnecessary and often wrong interpretation of religion's effect on the commitment of its adherents to doing something about the human world around them. The American psychiatrist Robert Coles and his wife Jane Hollowell Coles have spent many years getting to know migrant workers and other poor Americans, especially in the Appalachian region. Many of the people interviewed by the Coleses testify to how religious faith may strengthen them to struggle for a better life for themselves here and now. For example, one woman, a native of Harlan County, Kentucky,

> told her daughter that we are all lucky; that as the ministers keep saying, we are human beings, not animals, not stones, not trees, not metal—not pieces of potato, cut up and burning and soon enough eaten up. We have a will, a fate, a destiny. Heaven is a possibility; Hell is no one's inevitability—given a change of heart, an effort of the mind.

Thereupon the mother turns to her daughter and urges her to a very practical earthly "effort of mind": "You stay here and become a nurse. You be a proud woman of Harlan County who has learned to become a proud woman of Dayton."[7]

If a disciple of Jesus stops praying, it means that she or he has stopped putting hope in the power of God at work "on earth as it is in heaven." Not to pray is to abandon humans to their own devices, as if the God and Father of Jesus no longer cared or no longer could do anything to save us from ourselves. To resist this first temptation, Christians will need also to resist a second.

2. To forget Jesus. The book of Hebrews saw this as a danger in the very first generation of disciples. The good news, on which our faith depends, is not a disembodied religious idea. It is a reality embodied in the life, death, and resurrection of Jesus of Nazareth. The letter to the Hebrews is written to Christians subject to persecution. In all danger to your life and limb, the writer tells the church,

Consider him who endured from sinners such hostility against himself, so that you may not grow weary or fainthearted. (Hebrews 12:3)

For because he himself has suffered and been tempted, he is able to help those who are tempted. (Hebrews 2:18)

In American church history, no part of the Christian movement has understood such temptation, or resisted it with more integrity, than the churches of Black people. Their "spirituals"—songs composed in the eighteenth and nineteenth centuries in protest against their enslavement—abounded with references to Jesus, what he endured, and how his endurance strengthens his disciples for their own. "Nobody knows the trouble I've seen, nobody knows but Jesus." God's great gift to us for our resistance to temptation is Jesus our brother *in* temptation. Consider him! Then you will know that "nothing in all creation . . . can separate us from the love of God in Christ Jesus our Lord" (Rom. 8:39, NEB).

3. To forget the rest of the church. Every local congregation of Christians in history has been tempted by localism. During his ministry Paul was constantly reminding the new churches of Greece and Asia Minor that they were linked, through one gospel and one Holy Spirit, to sisters and brothers in Jerusalem and Rome. Today faithful Christians in South Korea tell us how important it is for them to know that others are praying for them in the midst of much official harassment by their government. In contrast, one spiritual difficulty borne by the Christians of China and by the rest of the world churches has been their separation from each other during the thirty years following the socialist revolution in that country in 1947. How tempting for *any* isolated band of believers to forget that they are sustained by the prayers of innumerable other members of the great church. During a visit to North India in 1953, I talked via translator with a group of outcaste Christians in a village. Having just attended a world conference of Christian young people, I tried to share with them the stories of Christians suffering for their faith in East Germany, South Africa, and the United States. "We feel better hearing about these things," they said to me simply. "It makes us feel less alone."

"Never cease to love your fellow Christians" (Heb. 13:1, NEB), to be grateful for them, and to pray with them!

Three Political Temptations

1. To confuse the causes of the church with the causes of God. We may call this a "political" temptation because it so often occurs when the church has some cause to promote in collision with the causes of secular society. The spiritual side of this temptation is the equation of things churchly and religious with the things of God. When, at the Constitutional Convention of 1787, American politicians like James Madison were proposing a real separation of "church" and "state," some religious people were sure that this would be a defeat of church contribution to future public life in America. Not so, said Madison: to relate church power and government power too closely is to risk losing the distinction between God and human institutions. The integrity of both government and the Christian gospel is at stake, said Madison. If we ask for official support of a religion by a government, we risk the implication that some "civil magistrate is a competent judge of truth or that he may employ religion as an engine of civil policy. The first is an arrogant pretension ... the second is an unhallowed perversion of the means of salvation."[8]

The kingdom of God is *not* synonymous with either human governments or human churches. Such heresy is old and tempting in world history. One thinks, for example, of tax exemptions for church schools—a policy that some citizens would base on the "free exercise of religion" clause of the U.S. Constitution—and then one reflects that, for a generation now, the phrase "Christian schools," in many parts of the country, has translated implicitly into the meaning: "private segregated education for white children in defiance of federally-ordered desegregation of public schools." Theologically alert Christians will always raise skeptical eyebrows about their own and others' blanket claims about "following the will of God." We are a people who pray regularly and by contrast, "Thy will be done"! But so praying, we have reason to question ourselves and others about our ethical priorities for society: who follows the will of God that humans should love their neighbors as persons like themselves—the segregators or the desegregators of American society? Who "does justice and loves mercy" with most integrity—those who open the doors of economic opportunity to all citizens or those who open the doors only to those with money to pay? If we cannot answer those questions absolutely, we must at least ask them.

The causes of both churches and governments will always be afflicted with ambiguity and short-fall from the "glory of God" (cf. Rom. 5:8). Self-doubt and perpetual timely repentance are the reverse, human side of real faith in the ultimate triumph of God's kingdom on earth: if the church in history had remembered that more consistently, it would not fall prey to the idea that "God wills it"—the Crusades, or a Thirty Years War or a World War, this or that Constitutional amendment, or the nuclear annihilation of the Soviet Union. In his teachings about God's ultimate purposes in our history, Jesus is clear that his disciples must resist premature certainty about divine presence in this or that human cause. Let "moral majorities" left and right, political activists of both liberal and fundamentalist persuasion, General Assemblies and Councils of churches, *every* self-styled "righteous remnant" learn humility in politics! And let them base that humility on the knowledge of their own sins and the cautionary word of Jesus:

> "Take care that no one misleads you. For many will come claiming my name and saying, 'I am the Messiah'; and many will be misled by them. The time is coming when you will hear the noise of battle near at hand and the news of battles far away; see that you are not alarmed. Such things are bound to happen; but the end is still to come." (Matthew 24:4–6, NEB)

Hallow the name of God by refusing to identify that name with ephemeral human causes. Stand aside from that temptation! The end is still to come!

2. To fear or hate secular powers. We are to fear and hate demonic,
superhuman powers. In conformity with the thirteenth
chapter of *Revelation*, we rightly discern that, on some occasions,
a devil seems to have taken charge of this or that portion of
human history. But in conformity with the thirteenth chapter of
Romans, we are to resist the easy identification of the secular
world with the realm of the devil. As a rule, we are to treat the
"powers that be" as neighbors and creatures like ourselves, as
part of social structures devised by humans and inhabited by all
of us.

For example, in the East African country of Kenya, in the
year 1970, a great political crisis swept through a large part of
the Presbyterian Church there. The party in power in the government decided that it would force all its supporters to take
part in an "oathing ceremony" in Nairobi, reminiscent of an
ancient tradition in the Kikuyu tribe. Ministers of the Presbyterian Church in East Africa include many Kikuyu. They resist,
on Christian principle, such ceremonies as the ancient Christians resisted, burning incense before the bust of Caesar. One
such minister, Jacob Mugo, pastor of a church in Nakuru, was
visited one Saturday morning by a government soldier who
pointed a gun to his face and shouted, "Come with me to Nairobi, or I will shoot you dead." "Then you will have to shoot
me," said Mugo quietly, "but I would rather you came into my
kitchen and had a cup of tea with me." Surprised, the soldier sat
down to tea. In the conversation, the minister explained why he
could not cooperate even though he was a loyal Kenyan citizen.
Somewhat abashed, the soldier went on his way. Later he was
heard to say about Rev. Mugo, "When I die, that is the man I
want to conduct my funeral."

Fear and hatred of secular powers is as little appropriate to
Christian faith as worship of the same. The double rule of New
Testament ethics for the Christian's relation to government
seems to be: obey government when, in its ordinary usual work,
it serves public good as "God's servant" (Rom. 13:4); disobey it,
when, in its perversion from its role in the kingdom of God, it
poses as God or claims the right to be worshiped and to destroy

the opponents of its idolatry (Rev. 13:15). The latter case "is a call for the endurance and faith of the saints" (Rev. 13:10), a resistance to death of idolatry in its political form. The former, more ordinary case, is a call for spiritual-political aplomb: neither intimidation by, nor contempt for, the powers that control the law, the gun, the wealth of human society. For we are the children of one who rules the rulers of the world.

3. *To believe that God has forsaken some part of the world.* As the church composed the earliest of its creeds—the so-called Apostles Creed—the major theological enemies inside and outside the church were proponents of some doctrine of radical evil. The Marcionites, for example, saw the created world as evil. They tore the Old Testament, with its Creator, out of the Christian Bible. Certain Gnostics saw parts of humanity sunk hopelessly in the evil of "the flesh." For them true religion consisted in a struggle of the soul to get free of the flesh. The early church creeds all rejected these views and rejected them decisively. Such views, intellectually and spiritually, were temptations to be resisted; for to accept them was to sever the connection between God the Redeemer, God the Spirit, and God the Creator. It was to abandon large parts of reality to the dominion of some other lord than the one to whom Jesus prayed. It was to pour contempt upon the fleshly humanity of Jesus himself and to suggest that the flesh was worth neither loving nor saving. Against this the Apostles Creed cried out, "I believe in God the Father Almighty, Maker of heaven and earth, And in Jesus Christ His only Son . . . who was . . . *born* of the Virgin Mary, *suffered* under Pontius Pilate, was *crucified, dead,* and *buried*; . . . And the third day he rose again from the dead . . ." [emphasis added]. He identified himself with every dimension of a full human life from womb to tomb! Now it can truly be believed that "nothing shall separate us from the love of God in Jesus Christ our Lord" (Rom. 8:39). Now we can expect to find the Spirit of God at work in any corner of this creation.

This was not an easy belief in the first century. Neither is it in the twentieth. Perhaps it is especially difficult in the twenti-

eth, since few centuries have been so full of such massive evil.
Elie Wiesel, a Jew born in Romania who as a young boy suffered
the horrors of a German concentration camp, tells the story of a
twelve-year-old boy about to be executed for some minor viola-
tion of a rule in the camp at Auschwitz. As they stood in the
yard watching the hanging, one Jew whispered to another,

> "Where is God now?"
> And I heard a voice within me answer him:
> "Where is He? Here He is—He is hanging on this gallows. . . ."[9]

Such faith does honor to both the Jewish and the Christian
understanding of God. Nothing tests that faith more severely
than the evils that haunt the political history of the world. Does
God really guide the world through a Cuba crisis? If the Chi-
nese Communists had banished the church from their society,
would that have banished God? Was the enslavement of millions of Black people in early American history an evil unre-
deemed and unnoticed by the God who redeemed and noticed
the sufferings of Egyptian slaves? Was the Nazi almost-
successful attempt to destroy the Jewish people the final put-
down of belief in *that* God?

We Christians have no naive, spiritually or politically glib
answer to these questions. Our best answer is still an answer of
practical, practicing faith. Again, as in all basic theology, it is a
matter of what part of our history and experience we trust as
the clue to all the other parts. Whose witness is the key? that of
the slave traffickers? that of Heinrich Himmler? or Jesus and all
his witnesses?

> Since we are surrounded by so great a cloud of witnesses, let us
> also lay aside every weight, and sin which clings so closely, and
> let us run with perseverance the race that is set before us, look-
> ing to Jesus the pioneer and perfecter of our faith, who for the
> joy that was set before him endured the cross, despising the
> shame, and is seated at the right hand of the throne of God.
> (Hebrews 12:1–2)

—where that God, in the name of that Jesus, still hears our
prayers.

Our Final Deliverance from Evil to Come

In the early nineteen-sixties the uncanny imagination of Fernando Krahn pictured two eras of western history, both having to do with belief in angels and devils. In an upper cártoon panel, Krahn portrays a medieval battlefield where two knightly armies are clashing. High above, angels and devils hover, superintending their chosen sides of the human battle. A lower cartoon panel shifts to the twentieth century. We see only the feet of a line of human soldiers. Around the human feet are gathered, in pygmy array, the figures of angels and devils.[10]

Scholars incline to the view that "the evil" in Matthew's version of the Lord's Prayer should be interpreted, "the evil one," that is, the Satanic power. Belief in angelic powers—good and evil—does not come easily to many twentieth-century Christians, but belief in evil comes easily enough. Have we not just catalogued enough horror from the past seventy years of human history to surfeit seven hundred years, or the whole of that history? What fear can we have of "the evil one" when human deviltry seems well equipped now to design chemical warfare, death camps, and nuclear genocide? As defenders of earth's fragile ecology have recently reminded us, next to volcanoes human beings are the most destructive things on earth; and we have it in our power now to exceed the power of the volcanoes. Was the development of the human brain an evolutionary "mistake"? Our answer to the question must not be theoretical but political: if the twentieth century is to graduate into the twenty-first century without nuclear holocaust, we will have to evolve quickly towards new levels of global humility and repentance. But as a recollection of chapter 1 of this book will suggest, underneath our willingness to repent must be a revival of our human sense of significance. The crisis of the late twentieth century is best phrased (as Kenneth Patchen puts it drolly) not in the question "Do we believe in God?" but in the question: "Does God believe in us?"[11] That is another way of asking: are we worth believing in? Who are these humans, "that thou art mindful" of them? (Ps.8:4).

The temptation to equate the human story to "a tale told by an idiot, full of sound and fury, signifying nothing," is old and strong. Our huge scientific, technical, and political achievements may obscure the crisis of self-confidence that haunts these days of our years on earth. But it feeds the crisis too. Is there an insidious, anonymous evil at work in our midst here? C. S. Lewis has his arch-devil Screwtape reflect that "our policy, for the moment, is to conceal ourselves."[12] While Lewis' wry fantasies of demonry may be no argument for the reality of "personalized evil," he does alert us to the ordinary truth that evil is a great masquerader in human affairs. When he joined the company of those who were plotting to assassinate Adolf Hitler, Dietrich Bonhoeffer was convinced that Hitler was a peculiar embodiment of evil, the "Anti-Christ." For Bonhoeffer the battle between the Divine and the demonic was taking place right there in Nazi Germany. Many an allied soldier who broke through the barbed wire of the death camps at the end of World War II must also have felt confronted with powers of darkness in the corpses and hollow-eyed survivors. What then shall we say about the powers that have concocted fifty thousand atomic warheads on missile launchers across the earth, readied for the destruction of vast numbers of us? If one were among the humans to survive such a disaster, might one not look on the ruins of whole countries with a shivering new sense that the devil really does exist?

The end of human life on earth is not the evil that heaves into sight here. The evil consists in the human will and capacity to bring about an end, in an evil time, before God's good time, before the story God wills to tell through us is finished. If we managed to finish it prematurely, would that mean the utter frustration of God's purposes on earth? The biblical faith does not permit us to say so. Even if human life came to an end tomorrow on this planet, it is still the planet made by a loving Creator; still the place where a human creature came under divine tutelage in the knowledge of good; still the habitat of many sons and daughters of Abraham; still the scene of divine purpose for a people liberated from their overlords in Egypt;

still the earth where a man from Nazareth taught disciples to be human by teaching them to pray, "Our Father. . . ." Whatever twentieth-century humans do to wreck the human story, what God has written to date in that story remains permanently worth telling about, to ears that may be waiting in other parts of this wondrous universe!

Whether or not we decide to speak of the "power of evil" or "the evil power," the fact remains that in our time we have much negotiation with evil too powerful for our powers. In his teachings Jesus predicts that, down to the end of human history and especially at the end, this battle will continue. Quite aside from latter-day Christian prophets who pretend to know the details of the "final battle" between God and Satan, Jesus does teach his disciples to anticipate struggles against temptation and evil, repeatedly in their lifetimes, but climactically at the "end of days." Revelation 3:10 contains the promise of the risen Lord: "Because you have kept my command and stood fast, I will also keep you from the ordeal that is to fall upon the whole world and test its inhabitants" (Rev. 3:10, NEB). As Raymond E. Brown says, in his consistently future-oriented interpretation of the Lord's Prayer, Jesus prays for his disciples (in John 17:15) that the Father "shouldst keep them from the evil one," and again in Gethsemane he urges the disciples to "pray that you may be spared the test," (*peirasmos* Mark 14:38, NEB), the great test to which the evil one will finally subject the whole earth. Brown summarizes this last petition of the Lord's Prayer: "Faced with the awesome power of the strong one, the Christian begs for the help of a stronger"[13] (Matt. 12:28–29). God is that stronger one, in whom Jesus trusted and by whom he was raised from the dead.

As we have seen, neither the New Testament texts of the Lord's Prayer nor the experiences of the church in history permit us to neglect either the dailiness or the ultimate future of Christian discipleship. We are called to live "between the times." We know what the ultimate future is about, though we have no knowledge of its details. In the midst of the details that make up each day of our lives, we strive for an obedience so consistent with that ultimate future that the Lord will honor it in that very day. Then, to those who learned from him to pray like this, he will announce that this prayer has been answered for ever and ever: "Come, O blessed of my Father, inherit the kingdom prepared for you from the foundation of the world!"

Notes

Introduction

1. Helmut Thielicke, *Our Heavenly Father*, trans. John W. Doberstein (New York: Harper and Brothers, 1960), 157.

2. E. F. Scott, *The Lord's Prayer* (New York: Charles Scribner's Sons, 1951), 52.

3. Karl Barth, *Prayer According to the Catechisms of the Reformation*, trans. Sara F. Terrien (Philadelphia: Westminster Press, 1952), 13.

4. The Christian Literature Society, Box 501, Park Town, Madras 600 003. This book, available only in India, has its origin in an invitation extended to me by the Rt. Rev. Thomas Mar Athanasius Suffragan, Metropolitan and by His Grace Most Rev. Dr. Alexander Mar Thoma, Metropolitan. It is with their permission and that of the Christian Literature Society that portions of this earlier book have been used in the present one. In addition, my earliest attempt to think along these lines can be found in the article, "The Prayer That Spans the World: An Exposition: Social Ethics of the Lord's Prayer," *Interpretation*, Vol. XXI, No. 3, (July 1967): 274–288.

Chapter 1

1. I am told by experts in Russian culture that the phrase "God will not forgive us" is a colloquialism not far from casual reference to "le bon Dieu" among the French or the exclamation "God help us!" among the English and Americans. The point is not to catch a Marxist believing in God but rather to note that the marks of prayer lie deep in the cultures of the world.

2. Cf. Matthew 6:7 and John 1:14.

3. Because the words of the prayer in Matthew 6:9–13 and Luke 11:1–4 vary significantly, scholars have long wondered which of

the two texts were closest to the prayer which Jesus first taught. Raymond E. Brown summarizes a very carefully researched answer to this question as follows:

> It is generally held that the short Lucan form most closely represents in the number of its petitions the form of the prayer as historically spoken by Jesus. The principle behind this solution is that it would be very difficult to conceive that the Lucan tradition would have dared to excise petitions from a longer form, for the prayer, being Jesus' own, took on a sacred character which would have discouraged such omissions. It is much more likely that the Matthean tradition represents a prayer to whose original petitions have been joined other sayings of Jesus. . . .
>
> However, we now recognize that the case of [the Lord's Prayer] was probably not a simple matter of literary editing. We are dealing with a prayer that was recited frequently by the early Christians and thus became a part of the Christian liturgy. Therefore what Matthew may well be giving us in Greek is the form of the [Lord's Prayer] recited in the churches of Syria (it is with this area that the first Gospel is usually associated). Here the Aramaic tongue of Jesus was the spoken language. . . .
>
> On the other hand, while Luke's tradition preserves the shorter and more original outline, the Gentile churches whose tradition Luke represents have also had their influence. The wording of the Lucan petitions has been adapted to their use, understanding, and outlook. . . .

"The Pater Noster as an Eschatological Prayer," in *New Testament Essays* (New York: Paulist Press, Reprint 1982), 218–220. On this latter adaptation see also p. 42.

4. In the Greek text of Matthew 6:9–13, there are fifty-seven Greek words, nine of which make reference to "us" or "our." Luke's briefer version contains thirty-eight Greek words, seven of which do so. By any count, in so short a prayer, this is a high percentage of "usness."

5. The word "church" is a Christian invention. It was related, from early centuries of the Christian movement, to the Greek word *kurios*, "Lord." The ordinary New Testament word for the Christian community is *ekklesia* "assembly," a group of people "called out" for some purpose. The less ordinary word "church" puts emphasis on the one who did the calling.

6. Cf. Ernst Troeltsch, *The Social Teaching of the Christian Churches*, trans. Olive Wyon, 2 vols. (London: George Allen and Unwin,

1931), 1: chapter 1; Charles N. Cochrane, *Christianity and Classical Culture* (New York: Oxford University Press, Galaxy Books, 1957); and Erich Auerbach, *Mimesis: The Representation of Reality in Western Literature*, trans. Willard Trask (Garden City, N.Y.: Doubleday, 1957). Copyright 1953 by Princeton University Press. The quotation from Auerbach is from pp. 37–38.

7. Cf. Deuteronomy 32:5, 2 Samuel 7:14, 1 Chronicles 17:13, 22:10, 28:6; Isaiah 9:6; Psalms 27:10, 68:5, 89:26, 103:13; Jeremiah 3:3–4, 3:19, 31:9; Malachi 1:6, 2:10. Robert Hamerton-Kelly observes that the term "Our Father" was coming into Jewish liturgical use during Jesus' lifetime, in contrast to Old Testament liturgical precedent. Nonetheless "this invocation does not indicate a personal intimacy with God of the kind which is the hallmark of Jesus' use of 'father' in his prayers." Most strikingly, "while our evidence shows that the Jews of Jesus' world would never address God as *'abba'*, Jesus always did!" The only exception in the Gospels to this "always" is Jesus' agonized address to God, "My God, My God. . . ," which is a quotation from Psalm 22:1. Robert Hamerton-Kelly, *God the Father* (Philadelphia: Fortress Press, 1979), 54, 72.

8. See also Matthew 26:39 and Luke 22:42. Matthew has the phrase "my Father" frequently on Jesus' lips (forty-two times); Luke has it occasionally (fifteen); John has it superabundantly (one hundred and nine); and Mark has it hardly at all (four). It is the more remarkable, then, that Mark (the earliest-written Gospel narrative) alone repeats literally that Aramaic address, *abba* in the Gethsemane prayer. Apparently only two other Aramaic words entered the ordinary liturgy of the New Testament churches: *amen* ("so be it") and *maranatha* ("Our Lord, come," 1 Cor. 16:22).

9. James McBride Dabbs, *The Road Home* (Philadelphia: Christian Education Press, 1960), 38.

10. Max C. Otto, *Science and the Moral Life* (New York: New American Library, Mentor Books,1949), 137.

11. Wilbur Daniel Steele, "The Man Who Saw Through Heaven," in *A World of Great Stories*, ed. Hiram Haydn and John Cournos (New York: Crown Publishers, 1947), 45–58.

12. This is a phrase I have frequently heard in the worship of Black Protestant churches in this country. It is consistent with Jesus' own way of calling to that positive side of our always-threatened existence: "You do live. Your strength to do so, you owe to God, in this very moment."

13. H. Richard Niebuhr, *Christ and Culture* (New York: Harper and Brothers, 1951), 17.

14. The earliest non-biblical reference to the Lord's Prayer appears in the Apostolic writing called *Didache* or "The Teaching of the Twelve Apostles," which scholars now date as almost contemporary with the writing of the New Testament—not later than A.D. 100 (cf. Brown, "Pater Noster," 218). *Didache* gives a version of the prayer close to Matthew's and includes the Doxology (see p. 90.) The quotation of the prayer, in *Didache* 8:2, comes just after instructions for the conduct of the baptismal ceremony (7:1–4) and just before instruction for the Lord's Supper (9:1–5), suggesting that the prayer was liturgically located between the two rituals in the early church. *Didache* 8:3 instructs Christians, "three times a day, pray thus," indicating that the Lord's Prayer was widely and frequently in use and that it was used for prayer at home as well. Text from Edgar J. Goodspeed, *The Apostolic Fathers: An American Translation* (New York: Harper and Brothers, 1950), 14–15.

15. Joachim Jeremias, *The Lord's Prayer*, trans. John Reumann (Philadelphia: Fortress Press, Facet Books, 1964), 19–20. I can personally testify that "children can say *'abba'*" who cannot very well say the English word "father." Our three children attempted to say "father" in forms that came out (respectively among the three) "awa," "favver," and "wavver"! The sounds in all of these words are chiefly labials, using lip and front-of-the-mouth muscles, as also in the words "mama" and "poppa."

16. J. B. S. Haldane, *Possible Worlds: And Other Papers*, facsimile ed. (Salem, New Hampshire: Ayer Co., S. A. Index Reprint Series, 1928).

17. Phyllis Trible, review of Robert Hamerton-Kelly, *God the Father*, (cited above, note 7), in a pre-publication copy, November 1982, 9–10.

18. Presbyterians, not reputed in some quarters as prayerful or spiritually open in their theological "style," have often heard from their pulpits the classic story from the Westminster Assembly of 1643–45, how one of its members contributed, in an hour-long prayer, to the language which the Assembly eventually adopted for defining the Sovereign God of Calvin and the Bible. Rushing to look at his "notes" for that prayer, assembly members found the single repeated phrase: *"Da lucem, Domine"* ("Give light, O Lord"). In a time of much scholasticism in Protestant theology, this dependence upon prayer as a matrix and door to new theological statements was remarkable. As one recent Lutheran historian has said of the Westminster Assembly, "That so many learned and conten-

tious men in an age of so much theological hairsplitting could with so little coercion establish so resounding a consensus on so detailed a doctrinal statement is one of the marvels of the century." Sydney E. Ahlstrom, *A Religious History of the American People*, 2 vols. (Garden City, N.Y.: Doubleday and Co., 1975), 1:136.

19. In her groundbreaking book, *God and the Rhetoric of Sexuality* (Philadelphia: Fortress Press, 1978), Professor Trible shows how the Old Testament uses female imagery to describe God more often than we tend to remember in the contemporary church. Cf. Hosea 11:1–4; Numbers 11:11–12; Isaiah 49:15; Isaiah 66:10–13; and Deuteronomy 32:18. All but the first passage have direct, unmistakably female images for God without any suggestion that Yahweh's relation to Israel, after the pattern of Canaanite religion, is that of a mythological ancestor.

20. Catharina Halkes, "The Themes of Protest in Feminist Theology Against God the Father," in *God as Father?*, ed. Johannes-Baptist Metz and Edward Schillebeeckx (New York: Seabury Press, 1981), 109.

21. Hamerton-Kelly, *God the Father*, 60–61.

22. Halkes, "Themes of Protest," 108. The allusions to Rosemary Ruether taken here from Halkes, 106–107, are from Ruether's book *Sexism and God-talk: Toward a Feminist Theology* (Boston: Beacon Press 1983).

23. Madeleine Boucher, Phyllis Trible, and Janet Walton, "A Brief Statement of the Theological Problem of Sexist Language," Union Theological Seminary, November 1982, 3.

24. Cf. Erik H. Erikson, *Childhood and Society*, 2nd. ed. (New York: W. W. Norton and Co., 1963), 249–250, and *Young Man Luther* (New York: W. W. Norton and Co., 1958), 118–119, where he remarks: "Of all the ideological systems . . . only religion restores the earliest sense of appeal to a Provider, a Providence. In the Judeo-Christian tradition, no prayer indicates this more clearly than 'The Lord make His face to shine upon you and be gracious unto you. The Lord lift up His countenance upon you and give you peace'; and no prayerful attitude better than the uplifted face, hopeful of being recognized."

25. Martin Buber, *Between Man and Man* (London: Routledge and Kegan Paul, 1947), 51.

26. Among the references here are Matthew 11:25; John 5:17; Matthew 5—7 *passim*; Matthew 16:17, 18:10, 20:23, 23:9, 25:34, 26:29, 26:42, 26:53; Luke 23:46, 24:49; and Matthew 28:19.

27. Thomas Wolfe, *You Can't Go Home Again* (New York: Harper & Row Publishers, Inc., 1934), 103.

28. "Epilogue: An Interpretation of the Debate Among Black Theologians," eds. Gayraud S. Wilmore and James H. Cone in *Black Theology: A Documentary History, 1966–1979* (Maryknoll, N.Y.: Orbis Books, 1979), 619–620.

29. See p. 83.

30. Walther Luthi, *The Lord's Prayer*, trans. Kurt Schoenenberger (Richmond: John Knox Press, 1961), 6–7.

Chapter 2

1. These quotations are from an informally circulated document "Europe Trip Report," by Howard Schomer, Secretary for Europe/World Issues of the United Church of Christ Board of World Ministries, New York City, Fall 1978.

2. See Robert T. Handy, *A Christian America: Protestant Hopes and Historical Realities* (New York: Oxford University Press, 1971).

3. The most thorough, astute raising of these questions among contemporary theological books is in H. Richard Niebuhr, *Christ and Culture* (cited above, note 13, chapter 1). A wider reading of this book might protect the members of American churches from the excesses of glib patriotism and acclaim for all-things-American that make some of them vulnerable to such movements as the Moral Majority.

4. Arthur Campbell Ainger, "God Is Working His Purpose Out," in *The Hymnbook* (Richmond: Presbyterian Church in the United States, The United Presbyterian Church in the U.S.A., Reformed Church in America, 1955), 500–501.

5. See Matthew 24:36. Good background for the question here can be gained by a reading of the two chapters, Matthew 24—25.

6. Ainger, "God Is Working . . . ," *The Hymnbook*, 500–501.

7. Brown, *New Testament Essays*, 253. Brown characterizes the Greek verb "give" in Luke's version of the petition for bread as "continuative and noneschatological," in contrast to the aorist verb in the Matthew version. (Ibid, 239.) See pp. 72–73.

8. Brown, ibid., 234; 227, note 36.

9. Cf. Bonhoeffer, *Letters and Papers from Prison*, ed. Eberhard Bethge, enlarged ed. (New York: The Macmillan Company, 1971), 310.

10. Cf. Luke 12:35–40; Matthew 24:36–51, 25:14–30; 1 Corinthians 4:1–5.

11. From the final declaration of the First Assembly of the World Council of Churches in Amsterdam, 1948. See "Findings and Decisions, First Assembly of the W.C.C.," (Geneva and New York: 1948), 10.

12. See p. 102.

13. Rome's distrust of "unlicensed" organizations of all sorts—what we would call voluntary associations—is well documented in the famous correspondence between the Emperor Trajan and his governor Pliny in Bithynia. (Trajan was emperor from A.D. 98–117.) The two Romans agree that if you let a few people assemble around so innocent sounding a cause as putting out fires—a volunteer fire department—their interest will soon turn to politics. Cf. this correspondence in "Christians in Bithynia" and "Trajan's Policy Towards Christians" in *Documents of the Christian Church*, ed. Henry Bettenson (New York: Oxford University Press, 1947), 5–7 and T. R. Glover, *The Influence of Christ in the Ancient World* (Cambridge: The University Press, 1929), 30–31.

14. Hedrick Smith, *The Russians* (New York: Ballantine Books, 1976), 90.

15. Cf. William Temple, *Nature, Man, and God* (London: Macmillan and Co., 1951), 148.

16. Luthi, *The Lord's Prayer*, 38.

17. The two words placing the word "bread" in a *time* frame, in the Lord's Prayer, are the subject of considerable scholarly perplexity into which I will not much enter here. What does Jesus mean by this double reference, "our daily bread today"? To account for the seeming redundancy, scholars have offered various translations of the word "daily" (*epiousion*) in Matthew 6:11 and Luke 11:3 (the only occurrences of the word in the entire New Testament), the phrase "each day" (*kath' hemeran*) in Luke 11:3, and the adverb "today" (*semeron*) in Matthew 6:11. The dispute has circled around the rare word, *epiousion*. Some say that the word really is a redundancy that underscores the pressing daily neediness of hungry people. Others conclude that the word is better translated "for our need," as though no time reference were intended. Yet others see the word as derived from the Greek word for "going" and "coming," so that the time reference is, "for the coming day, tomorrow." Those who adopt this interpretation may go on to conclude that the "coming day" is the day of the end-time, the final eschatologi-

cal banquet. A fine summary of all these possibilities can be found in Brown, *New Testament Essays*, 238–243. He adopts a fully eschatological interpretation. Following his admission that the Lucan version of the bread-petition lacks verbal suggestion of eschatological tension, I have opted for the more usual understanding that the petition, while perhaps allusive to Christian anticipation of the heavenly banquet, is inescapably concerned with the concreteness of that anticipation in today's bread-on-the-table.

18. Colin Turnbull, *The Mountain People* (New York: Simon and Schuster, Touchstone Books, 1972).

19. This was Oliver Wendell Holmes, Jr.'s pithy definition of real freedom of speech.

20. William Lee Miller, *The Protestant and Politics* (Philadelphia: The Westminster Press, 1958), 66.

21. In research reported in the book, *Is There Hope for the City?*, by Donald W. Shriver, Jr. and Karl A. Ostrom, (Philadelphia: Westminster Press, 1977), we document the claim that the people in American society who "keep their hopes up" are most likely to be the people who keep up their political involvements. Not to be carrying your hope for a better world into some political expression is to jeopardize your ability to continue entertaining such hope, we discovered. In interviews with almost a thousand carefully sampled people living in central North Carolina, we found that persons who believed in social justice for the poor, for example, but who shy away from political participation, are likely to resemble "tired liberals." People with continued, stubborn hope for justice in American society tended to be those who combined: (1) a strong religiously rooted faith with (2) strong relationships to supportive friends and (3) regular participation in some form of collective public life. Faith without political works withers; political works without faith and friends are short-winded. This says something striking and fundamental about an authentic Christian lifestyle: this lifestyle combines prayerful believing, social connection to fellow-believers in the church, and wide-ranging public service. In this connection, cf. two recent books: Parker J. Palmer, *The Company of Strangers* (New York: Crossroad Publishing Co., 1981) and Martin E. Marty, *The Public Church*, (New York: Crossroad Publishing Co., 1981). Strikingly similar empirical conclusions, parallel to those of *Is There Hope for the City?* can be found in a 1981 study sponsored by the Connecticut Mutual Life Insurance Company, "The Conneticut Mutual Life Report on American Values in the '80's: The Impact of Belief" (Hartford, 1981), 64–66.

22. Flora Lewis, "On a Collision Course," *The New York Times*, 10 August, 1982, editorial section.

23. A concrete illustration, related to Presbyterian Church missions, was India Village Service in North India in the 1940s and 1950s. The United Nations and the government of India modeled some of their village-development programs after this small project, organized by two American Presbyterian missionaries, Charlotte and William Wiser. See their book, *Behind Mud Walls* (New York: Agricultural Missions, Inc., 1951).

24. Here is one urban historian's summary of how the "trickle-down" system of housing supply-and-demand has worked in most American cities of this century: "Because the lower-income half of American urban families had to find their housing in the structures vacated by the upper half, the new environment of the 1880–1920 years is the old environment of today's cities. These former growth rings are now the gray areas of today's metropolis—the Brooklyns and Bronxes of New York, the West and South Sides of Chicago, the East Sides and Hamtramcks of Detroit." Sam Bass Warner, *The Urban Wilderness* (New York: Harper & Row, 1972), 205. The economics and sociology of southern cities betray exactly the same syndrome.

25. Lee A. Daniels, "Brooklyn Churches Gain City Help for New Homes," *The New York Times*, 30 July 1982. Section B.

26. These verses follow the opening verses of Isaiah 61, as Jesus quotes them in the famous Nazareth synagogue announcement of the beginning of his ministry (Luke 4:16–19). In its full Isaianic context (Isa. 61:1–4), the messianic mission connects, in a broadly comprehensive way, what modern versions of the biblical ethic have often split apart (cf. Introduction, p. 1.). Here are the many dimensions of ministry: preaching ("bring good tidings to the afflicted"), social service ("opening the prison to those who are bound"), eschatological anticipation ("proclaim the year of the Lord's favor and the day of our God"), pastoral comfort ("to comfort all those who mourn"), spiritual joy ("the mantle of praise"), and social-political reconstruction ("repair the ruined cities"). This is a stunning evocation of the wholistic biblical perspective on what God intends as the work of a "chosen people" in the world at large. Seldom do either fundamentalist or liberal theologies of our time come up to this standard.

27. Matthew 25:32. Note that "nations," not just a collection of individuals, are "gathered before" the Son of Man.

Chapter 3

1. "The Address to Diognetus," in *The Apostolic Fathers*, trans. Edgar J. Goodspeed, (New York: Harper and Brothers, 1950), 278. This was probably written in the third century.

2. Augustine, *The City of God*, trans. Marcus Dods, (New York: Random House, The Modern Library, 1950), XIX:271.

3. Charles N. Cochrane, *Christianity and Classical Culture*, 221–222.

4. S. McLean Gilmour, "Introduction ·ánd Exegesis" in *The Interpreter's Bible*, ed. George Arthur Buttrick, 12 vols. (New York: Abingdon Press, 1952), 8:408. See also Acts 7:60.

5. Along with R. E. Brown, the New Testament scholar Krister Stendhal also interprets the Lord's Prayer as thoroughly eschatological. With one exception, says Stendhal, all the "spiritual gifts" promised in the New Testament to Christians are delayed, partially experienced gifts. Only in the end will all these gifts come to God's people in their perfection. But the exception to this generalization is the experience of forgiveness in the Christian community. "Since their part in it (the age to come), as a community, presupposes true fraternal relations, the very right to utter such a prayer depends upon a status of mutual forgiveness." Stendhal, "Prayer and Forgiveness," *Svensk Exegetisk Arsbok*, (1958), 22—23:83.

6. "Youth Shot 'for Laughing' Dies: 2 Boys, 13 and 16, Are Arraigned," *The New York Times* ,7 July 1978. Section B.3.

7. It is also anthropological. Kant's great work, *Religion Within the Limits of Reason Alone*, clearly demonstrates the difficulty encountered by all theologians (and all philosophers who believe in God), of separating notions of the divine from notions of the human. Kant's "rational" God is an inference from the human experience of unqualified moral obligation—"the categorical imperative." God and humans are both at their best, so to speak, when they subject themselves to right moral intention. On this narrow base, Kant's theology yields a God who has to demand of humans all that they can do. He was not unaware of the human need for divine help or the biblical assurance of the same. But this awareness had no place in the logical straightjacket of his system. As John R. Silber says of the unremitting Kantian fidelity to the principle, "I ought, therefore I can": "If the individual has done all that he can, he does not need grace. And if he has not, even Kant agrees that he should not get it." (Introduction, *Religion Within the Limits of Reason Alone* (New York: Harper and Brothers, Harper Torchbooks, 1960, p. cxxxiii.) So, for Kant and partisans of this first objection to the forgiveness

of sins, forgiveness is either empirically irrelevant or morally impermissible. Quite missing from this classic discussion, however, is a sense of the social costs of such an ethic—as over against its cost to individual behavior. The human subject of all this discussion is the lonely individual. The horror of an *unforgiving society* little penetrates the debate.

8. O. Hobart Mowrer, *The Crisis in Psychiatry and Religion* (New York: D. Van Nostrand, Insight Books, 1961), 188–200. Mowrer also joins the third group of critics below.

9. James McBride Dabbs, *Who Speaks for the South?* (New York: Funk and Wagnalls, 1964), 252.

10. Robert Frost, "The Mending Wall" in *The Poetry of Robert Frost*, ed. Edward Connery Lathem (New York: Holt, Rinehart and Winston, 1979), 33–34.

11. George A. Buttrick, editor's Exposition of "The Gospel According to St. Matthew" in *The Interpreter's Bible*, 7:314.

12. Robert Short, *Something to Believe In* (New York: Harper & Row, 1978), 306.

Chapter 4

1. The Greek word *koinonia*, in its various New Testament settings, is often hard to translate accurately into English. "Fellowship" is a frequent rendering, but "participation" is often more accurate. It is a word associated in the New Testament epistles with the church and the continuing presence of the Spirit in the church, with strong associations with the linking of the community's members to one another and their risen Lord. Cf. 1 Corinthians 10:16 and 2 Corinthians 13:13, and L. S. Thornton, *The Common Life in the Body of Christ* (London: Dacre Press, 1950).

2. Cf. *Didache* 8:2.

3. Even today the *Pater Noster*, as said in the personal devotions of Roman Catholics, ends with the phrase "Deliver us from evil." But the public Mass of the church, at the point where the congregation is invited to pray the prayer with the priest, includes the doxology.

4. "Snatch us from the jaws of temptation" would be a translation close to the imagery of the Greek verb here. Cf. Karl Barth, *Prayer*, 74.

5. Jonathan Schell, *The Fate of the Earth* (New York: Alfred A. Knopf, 1982), 106.

6. Ibid., 95.

7. Robert Coles and Jane Hollowell Coles, *Women of Crisis: Lives of Struggle and Hope* (New York: Dell Publishing Co., Merloyd Lawrence Books, 1978), 126.

8. In Anson Phelps Stokes, *Church and State in the United States* (New York: Harper & Row, 1964), 57. It is worth noting that, in contrast to the skeptical and deist mindset of many framers of the United States Constitution, Madison, a student at John Witherspoon's Princeton, spoke and wrote on grounds of orthodox Christian claims. The quoted statement comes from Madison's long, carefully reasoned statement opposing the bill before the Virginia Legislature in 1785 to support with state funds the teaching of the Christian religion in the public schools.

9. Elie Wiesel, *Night* (New York: Avon Books, Discus Books, 1969), 76.

10. Editorial cartoon by Fernando Krahn in *The Reporter*, 8 October 1964.

11. Kenneth Patchen, *The Journal of Albion Moonlight* (New York: New Directions Publishing Corp., 1961), 10.

12. C. S. Lewis, *The Screwtape Letters* (New York: The Macmillan Co., 1948), 39.

13. Brown, *New Testament Essays*, 250–253.

Index

OF PERSONS AND SUBJECTS

Abba   8, 10ff., 21, 25–26, 30, 61
Ahlstrom, Sydney E.   113
  (n.18)
Analogy, in theology   19
Andropov, Yuri   5
Apostles' Creed   2, 103
Arabs   82
Argentina   67
Auerbach, Erich   9
Augustine   2, 41, 72 (n.2), 85
Authority; *see "Lordship"*

Banquet, heavenly   52, 55, 91
Barth, Karl   3 (n.3), 19, 92
Black Theology   31–32, 99
Bonhoeffer, Dietrich   43, 106
Bread, "daily,"   51–52, 115–116
  (n.17)
Brooklyn   65–66
Brown, Raymond E.   42, 43, 110
  (n.3)
Browning, Robert   28
Buber, Martin   30
Buttrick, George A.   118, 119
  (n.4, n.11)

Calvin   37
Calvinism   6, 20, 57
Capitalism   53, 58
"Christian America"   37, 50
Church
  context of prayer   7

Church (cont.)
  social expression of freedom
    46–49
  universal human community
    49–50
  advocate of justice in society
    50–69
  as "forgiven forgivers"
    87
  under persecution   89 ff.
Civil War, American   82
Cochrane, Charles N.   9, 72,
  75
Coles, Robert and Jane H.   98
Cone, James H.   31
Constantine   37, 48, 56
Corinth   8, 10
Crusades   101
Cuba Crisis   94–95, 104

Dabbs, James M.   13, 81
Didache   90, 112 (n.14)
Diognetus   71 (n.1)
Doxology   90–92

Economic systems   53
Ecumenical nature of Lord's
    Prayer   3–4;   *see also*
    "Church"
Erikson, Erik   28
Eschatology   39–44, 91–92,
    107–108, 115–116 (n.17)

Exodus   15–16, 20, 46, 104,
    106

"Father"; see "abba"
Feminism
  female images of God
      16–27
  in the church,   21, 22,
      23, 25
Food   45, 50–69; see "Hunger"
Forgiveness
  uniqueness   72, 75, 87
  vs. revenge   73–75, 79
  and justice   76–79
  and restitution   78–79, 86
  as reconciliation   79, 82, 85,
      87
  as liberation   83
  and "indignity"   84
  in the church   86–88
Freedom, of worship   48–50, 52,
    56
Freud, Sigmund   81
Frost, Robert   83

German Democratic Republic
    35, 58, 100
Government
  and idolatry   46–48, 103
  and justice   64
  as "God's servant"   102
Gnosticism   103

Haldane, J.S.B.   18
Halkes, Catherine   22, 24, 27
Hallowing the name of God   11,
    24, 47, 89, 101
Hamerton-Kelly, Robert   23
    (n.21)
Handy, Robert T.   37 (n.2)
Himmler, Heinrich   104
Hinduism   71, 82
Hiroshima   80–81
Hitler, Adolf   106

Holmes, O.W. Jr.   116
    (n.19)
Holy Spirit   16, 20, 25, 27, 32,
    48, 56, 61, 72, 89, 91, 92,
    93, 103
Housing   64–66
Hunger   14, 53–57

Idolatry   25, 46–49, 103
Ik   54
Imma   17, 21, 26
India   3, 50, 59, 71, 99–100
India Village Service   117 (n.23)
Intercession   99
Ireland   82

Jefferson, Thomas   50
Jeremias, Joachim   17, 112
    (n.15)
Jews, in World War II   82, 91,
    104
Justice   36, 50 ff., 56, 59, 61, 64,
    76, 78, 101
Justinian   37

Kaddish   91
Kant, Immanuel   118 (n.7)
Karma   71, 73, 79
Kenya   102
Kollwictz, Käthe   57
Korea, South   67–68, 99
Krahn, Fernando   105

Lewis, C.S.   106
Lewis, Flora   62
Liberation: social and religious
    49, 83
Lordship
  of Caesar   46
  of Jesus   47 ff.
  and "church"   110 (n.5)
Lord's Supper   15, 30
Luther, Martin   32, 44
Lüthi, Walter   33, 52

Madison, James 100
Male images of God 21–27
Marcion 28, 104
Mar Thoma Syrian Church 3, 64
Marxism 5, 35–38, 51
Marty, Martin 116 (n.21)
Materialism 43, 52
McEvoy, Leo 77–78
Mexico 62
Military budget 60–61
Miller, William Lee 116 (n.20)
Missionary movement 64
"Moral Majority" 101
Mother; see "Imma" and "Feminism"
Mowrer, O. Hobart 80
Mugo, Jacob 102

Naming of God 11–12, 26
"Nehemiah Plan" 65–66
Nicene Creed 2
Niebuhr, H. Richard 15, 114 (n.3)
Nuclear War 80–81, 94–97, 101, 105

Otto, Max C. 14
Ostrom, Karl A. 116 (n.21)

Palmer, Parker J. 116 (n.21)
Patchen, Kenneth 105
Paul, Pauline writings
  on social class 8–9
  on slavery 32
  on women in the church 21–22
  on forgiveness 73
Peter, Simon 9, 46, 93–94
Pliny 115 (n.13)
Politics 62 (n.21); see "Government," "Idolatry," and "Church"

Public vs. private religion 48, 62 (n.21)

Rauschenbush, Walter 60
Reagan, Ronald 63
Reconciliation; see "Forgiveness"
Resurrection of Jesus 15–16, 18, 29, 40, 46, 94, 98, 107
Robinson, John 20
Roman Empire 9, 41, 47 ff.
Ruether, Rosemary 23
Rusk, Dean 95

Satan, demonic powers 94, 102, 105, 106, 107
Saudi Arabia 62
Schell, Jonathan 96
Scott, E.F. 2
Separation of church and state 36, 100
Sermon on the Mount 6
Sexism; see "Feminism"
Slavery 8–10, 32, 80, 104
Smith, Hedrick 51
Social Class 8–9
Social nature of prayer; see "Church"
Socialism 35, 51, 53, 58, 59, 99
South Africa 67, 100
Soviet Union 5, 51, 58
Sri Lanka 68
Starvation 55
Steele, Wilbur Daniel 14
Stendhal, Krister 118 (n.5)
Syrian Orthodox Church 64

Temple, William 52
Temptation 90–104
Ten Commandments 2
Theodosius 56
Thielicke, Helmut 2
Thirty Years War 101
Thornton, L.S. 119 (n.1)

Time-focus of Lord's Prayer; *see*
    "Eschatology"
Trajan   115 (n.13)
Trible, Phyllis   19
Troeltsch, Ernst   9
Trust, basic   28–30
Turnbull, Colin   54

Universalism of Gospel   9–10,
    32, 33; *see "Church"*

Voltaire   49
Vonnegut, Kurt   87

Ward, Barbara   58
Warner, Sam Bass   117 (n.24)
Westminster Assembly   112
    (n.18)

Westminster Confession   6, 20,
    95
Wiesel, Elie   104
Wiser, Charlotte and William
    117 (n.23)
Wolfe, Thomas   31
Woolman, John   32
World Council of Churches   45
    (n.11)
World War I   95
World War II   80–82, 84, 91,
    95, 104, 106
Worship; *see "Freedom"*

Yahweh   11, 21

Zimbabwe   50

Index
OF SCRIPTURE REFERENCES

Numbers	
11:11–12	113

Deuteronomy	
32:5	111
32:18	113

2 Samuel	
7:14	111

1 Chronicles	
17:13	111
22:10	111
28:6	111

Esther	
4:14	45

Psalms	
8:4	105
22:1	93
27:9–10	31, 111
68:5	111
89:26	111
103:13	111

Isaiah	
9:6	111
10:5	56
32:18	66
49:15	113

Isaiah (cont.)	
61:1–4	66, 117
63:16	12
64:8	12
66:10–13	113

Jeremiah	
3:3–4	111
3:19	111
31:9	111

Hosea	
11:1	11, 113
11:3	11, 113

Amos	
5:21–24	57

Micah	
6:8	62

Malachi	
1:6	111
2:10	111

Matthew	
4:1–11	92
5:13–14	61
5:23–24	57
5:25	73
5:38–42	74

Matthew (cont.)		Luke (cont.)	
5:43–48	74	14:15–24	56
6:9	4	15:28	74
6:9–13	6	22:29–30	52
6:11	115	22:42	111
6:14–15	72	22:43–46	93
6:26–30	15	23:34	74
12:28–29	107	23:46	94
16:23	93		
18:32	74	**John**	
24:34	41	1:9	9
24:4–6	101	1:14	1, 52
24:11–30	115	3:21	3
24:36	42	17:15	107
25:31–46	42, 44, 52, 57, 117		
25:34	40, 67, 88, 108	**Acts**	
25:35	52	1:1	22
26:39	111	2:32	15
26:41–49	73	2:36	47
27:43	29	2:42	90
27:46	93	4:13	46
		4:29	90
Mark		7:60	90
1:12–13	92	10:1–48	56
1:15	41	16:13–15	21
2:5	74	16:25	30
3:31–35	23	17:22	5
14:36	12	18:1–4	21
14:38	107		
15:34	93	**Romans**	
		3:23	85
Luke		5:8	101
4:1–2	92	8:15	12
4:16–19	117	8:16	16
4:18	24	8:18–25	72
5:20	74	8:21	27, 50, 83
6:20	26	8:23	61, 91
7:37	76	8:26	25
7:41, 48	74	8:35	31
10:33	74	8:39	16, 63, 99
10:38	42	13:4	102
11:1	2		
11:1–4	6, 115	**1 Corinthians**	
12:35–40	115	1:26	8

1 Corinthians (cont.)
1:28–30 10
2:6 41
4:1–5 115
10:13 95
10:16 119
12:26 68
14:34 22
16:22 111

II Corinthians
4:7 20
5:19 71, 87
13:13 119

Galatians
3:28 21
4:6 12

Ephesians
3:20 25
4:15 27
4:32 71, 85

1 Thessalonians
5:17 98

1 Timothy
2:11–12 22

Hebrews
2:9 29
2:18 99
11:13 63, 91
12:1–2 104
12:3 99
13:1 100

1 John
2:10–11 75
4:19 74

Revelation
2:7 62
3:10 107
13:10, 15 102–103